Syriac   Back ground to Bibl

Armaic   —   Bl

GORGIAS HANDBOOKS

Volume 7

The Bible
In The Syriac Tradition

Martin Zammit

'Enbe men Karmo Suryoyo

A Syriac Chrestomathy

The Bible
In The Syriac Tradition

SEBASTIAN BROCK

Second Revised Edition

GORGIAS PRESS
2006

First Gorgias Press Edition, 2006.

Copyright © 2006 by Gorgias Press LLC.

All rights reserved under International and Pan-American Copyright
Conventions. Published in the United States of America by Gorgias
Press LLC, New Jersey.

ISBN 1-59333-300-5

GORGIAS PRESS
46 Orris Ave., Piscataway, NJ 08854 USA
www.gorgiaspress.com

Printed and bound in India by Replika Press

TABLE OF CONTENTS

PREFACE

This volume brings together two rather different introductions to the Bible in the Syriac tradition. Part I originated as a correspondence course written for use at the St. Ephrem Ecumenical Research Institute (SEERI), in Kottayam (Kerala, India), and it was published by SEERI as a booklet under the title *The Bible in the Syriac Tradition* in 1988. This has now been updated where necessary and a completely new (and expanded) 'Select Bibliography' has been provided; this covers not only the Syriac Bible itself, but also provides some basic bibliography to go with chapters IV–VIII, which concern different aspects of its reception history.[1]

Part II started out as the last chapter in the third (and final) volume of *The Hidden Pearl: The Syrian Orthodox Church and its Ancient Aramaic Heritage*, which had been written to accompany three documentaries, published by TransWorld Film (Rome) in 2001. Since these volumes are essentially a work of *haute vulgarisation* footnotes were deliberately avoided; some basic annotation, however, was provided separately, for the benefit of more academic readers, in the Internet *Journal of Syriac Studies* entitled *Hugoye* 5:1 (2002) [syrcom.cua.edu/Hugoye; pp. 63–112 in the printed version of this number]. In the present book, however, text and annotation have been brought together, and the latter has been brought up to date where necessary. The title of the chapter in *The Hidden Pearl* had been 'The Bible in Syriac', but since this was so similar to the title of Part I, it has here been altered to 'The Syriac Bible'.

Inevitably there is a certain amount of overlap between Part I and Part II, especially towards the beginning, but since the basic material is presented in two rather different ways, it seemed preferable to leave both Parts as they originally stood, and to recommend that readers simply skip whatever might prove to be redundant to their particular requirements.

Sebastian Brock
Oxford, England

---

[1] I take the opportunity to thank the Revd. Dr Jacob Thekeparampil, Director of SEERI, for permission to reprint this work. It might be mentioned that an earlier updated edition was translated into Syriac by Dayroyo Awgen Aydin, and was published by the Gorgias Press (Piscataway, NJ) in 2002.

PART I:
THE BIBLE IN THE SYRIAC TRADITION

CHAPTER I

1. HOW DOES THE BIBLE REACH US?

When we read the Bible today we normally read it in a modern printed edition and in a modern translation, whether it be in English, or Malayalam, or some other language. It is worth reflecting how these printed editions and translations came into being: what lies behind them, and how do they influence our understanding of what the "Bible" contains and says?

Printed Bibles only go back to the sixteenth century. Previous to that Bibles had to be copied by hand, a laborious and slow process. The invention of printing had two important consequences for the Bible: in the first place, printing has made it possible for Bibles to be circulated much more widely and much more cheaply; and secondly, printing has helped to standardize the arrangement and contents of the Bible. We shall be looking at some of the consequences of this revolutionary invention below.

The manuscript Bible was rarely a complete Bible, for normally a biblical manuscript would only contain part of the Bible, such as the Gospels, or maybe the whole New Testament. Each book would be divided into chapters, but several different systems of chapter divisions were current; thus, for example, the chapter division in Syriac and in Greek manuscripts differs from that in our printed Bibles. The chapter division familiar to us today in printed Bibles in fact belongs to the Latin translation by Jerome, known as the Vulgate; though the system was only devised in the Middle Ages, it was adopted in the printed text of the Bible in all languages in the sixteenth century, and so this particular system has now become universal. Manuscript Bibles in languages other than Hebrew also lacked any form of verse division; our present verse divisions in the Old Testament derive from the Hebrew Bible, and these too were introduced into printed Bibles in all languages in the course of the sixteenth century. In the New Testament the verse divisions and numberings were first introduced in some of the first printed editions of the Greek text.

Manuscript Bibles in all languages except Hebrew were in book, or "codex," form. For purposes of study the Jews would also write out the Hebrew Bible in codex form, but for liturgical use in Synagogue they always wrote out the text on scrolls (a practice which still exists today). The scroll is in fact a much older invention than the codex. The codex only came to be widely used for literary texts in the early centuries of the Christian era, and it seems that Christians helped to popularize the new format by first employing it for writing out biblical texts in Greek. The codex has many advantages over the scroll: in particular, the codex is much easier to use, and it can hold very much more text than a scroll.

Before the invention of the codex people had invariably used the scroll; thus, for example, the biblical manuscripts in Hebrew found at Qumran (on the shore of the Dead Sea) are all in scroll form (they date from about the second century BC to the first century AD. This means that the original authors of the various biblical books will have first written their books down on scrolls, rather than in book form, or codices. This almost certainly applies to the authors of the New Testament books as well as to those of the Old Testament.

The biblical manuscripts from Qumran, which come from a collection of texts often known as the "Dead Sea Scrolls" are the oldest surviving biblical manuscripts in Hebrew. Most of them are very fragmentary, and the earliest complete biblical manuscripts in Hebrew date from very much later, from the tenth century.

The books of the Hebrew Bible (the Christian Old Testament) were translated by Jews into Greek in the third and second centuries BC. This collection of translations came to be known as the Septuagint (Seventy, *Shab'in*) since an early tradition claimed that the Pentateuch had been translated into Greek at Alexandria by seventy translators from Palestine. The Greek-speaking part of the early Church took over this translation from the Jews, and in due course the Jews themselves abandoned it. A few small fragments from the second and first centuries BC survive, but the earliest complete manuscripts are Christian ones of the fourth and fifth centuries and later.

Jews also translated the Hebrew Bible into Aramaic, and these translations are known today as the Targums. Fragments of a pre-Christian Aramaic translation of Job have been found at Qumran, but the main Targums which survive probably originated in the early centuries of the Christian era, and the manuscripts containing them are almost all late medieval (twelfth to sixteenth century). Jews may also have translated some books of the Bible into an Aramaic dialect resembling Syriac (Syriac originated as the local Aramaic dialect of Edessa), and these were then taken over by the early Syriac-speaking Christian community to form the beginnings of the Peshitta Old Testament. The earliest complete manuscript of the Syriac Old Testament belongs to the sixth or seventh century.

Modern translations of the Bible are made from particular editions of the Hebrew Old Testament and Greek New Testament. Surviving manuscripts of the Hebrew Bible have a remarkably uniform text, and so there is very little difference between one edition of the Hebrew Bible and another; it is likely that the precise form of the Hebrew text as we know it goes back to an authoritative edition produced about the end of the first century AD. Before that date there was evidently a certain amount of variation between different manuscripts.

In contrast to the Hebrew Bible, manuscripts of the Greek Old Testament (Septuagint) and the Greek New Testament may differ from one another considerably in details of wording, and so modern editors have used the earliest available manuscripts in order to provide their readers with a text as close as possible to the text written down by the original authors. This is by no means a simple task, and as a result different editions of the Greek New Testament will often have slightly different texts. In most cases these modern editions will differ in many small ways from sixteenth-century editions, whose editors mostly relied on rather late manuscripts. These differences are reflected in the various English translations: one can easily discover this by comparing a passage in the King James version, made in the seventeenth century, with any twentieth-century English translation.

As we shall see, manuscripts of the standard Syriac Bible are remarkably uniform in character; in this respect they are comparable to Hebrew biblical manuscripts, and unlike Greek ones.

2. BIBLICAL TRANSLATION, SOME GENERAL PROBLEMS

Fashions in biblical translation change over the course of time. Twentieth-century biblical translators approach their task very differently from the way in which the ancient translators went about their work. The aims and the self-understanding of ancient and of modern biblical translators were radically different. One can generalize and say that the ancient translator was oriented towards the original text, while the modern translator is oriented towards the reader. As a result of this different orientation the ancient translator translates with great deference towards the original text, striving to translate it "word for word," even if this may sometimes result in "nonsense translations." In contrast, the modern translator seeks to render the text intelligible to his reader and as a consequence he translates "sense for sense," rather than "word for word"; and he will avoid at all costs any nonsense translations. Ancient translations will thus tend to be more literal, and modern ones more free and interpretative. Within each type of translation, the more literal and the more free, there is in fact the possibility of great variety, as we shall see later on, in connection with the Syriac Bible.

Virtually all ancient biblical translations, into whatever language, are basically text-oriented rather than reader-oriented. When did biblical translation change its practice and become reader-oriented? Right up to the end of the European Middle Ages word for word translation remained the norm for biblical translation, and it was only in the sixteenth century that the practice changed. There are good reasons for linking this important shift with the invention of printing.

Before the invention of printing the main context in which the Bible was read was during church services, but after the invention of printing it became much more available to be read by individuals at home. Since many passages in the Bible are extremely obscure, this new situation gave rise to problems for the Church, all the more so since it coincided in time with the movement for reform in Europe. As long as the reading of the Bible was largely confined to the context of the liturgy the Church was able to

11

exercise its authority in matters of scriptural interpretation since biblical readings could be accompanied by homiletic explanation. Once, however, that the Bible had become readily available outside the liturgy there was no longer any means of control over how the Bible was to be interpreted, and in the course of the Reformation period in Europe all sorts of extravagant interpretations began to circulate. There were two main reactions to this abuse of the Bible at the time: the Roman Catholic Church tried to minimize the use of the Bible outside the context of church services, thus reducing the danger of misguided interpretation of the Bible by individuals. The Reformation Churches, on the other hand, dealt with the problem in quite a different way, by adopting a completely new attitude towards biblical translation itself: from the time of St. Jerome (late fourth century) to the end of the European Middle Ages (fifteenth century) the ideal aimed at by all biblical translators had been (as we have seen) a "word for word," rather than "sense for sense," rendering; this meant that, if the original text was obscure, the translator was content to pass the obscurity on the reader, leaving the matter of explanation to the preacher. At the Reformation the role of translator came to be joined, to some extent, to that of the preacher or expositor, and so the entire aim of the biblical translation changed: no longer did the biblical translator defer to the original text, rendering it word for word, instead, he saw his task as conveying to the reader his own understanding of what the biblical text meant. Accordingly, in the process of translating the Bible into the various European spoken languages of the time, the Reformers felt the need to be much more interpretative in their work of translation than earlier translators had been.

Virtually all modern biblical translations have inherited this changed attitude towards the task of the biblical translator, although modern translations are interpretative in very different ways from sixteenth-century European translations.

St. Jerome, who produced the revised Latin translation known as the Vulgate, was the first person to formulate the view that it was appropriate to translate the sacred text of the Bible "word for word," rather than "sense for sense." We can, however, see from the history of the early biblical translations that this ideal had already been put into practice long before his time. In the case of most ancient translations of the Bible we can observe the same course of events: the earliest translations into a particular language are rather inconsistent in character, since the translators lacked experience and precedent; before long, however, people noticed that there were differences between the original and the translation, and so they started to revise the original translation, brining it closer into agreement with the original. This process of revision might be repeated, or go on over a period of time. In every case we end up with an extremely literal rendering of the original text. This movement towards a more and more literal style of translation can be particularly well documented from the history of both the Greek and the Syriac Bible, for in both cases we have somewhat inconsistent styles of translation at the earliest stages followed by a series of revisions aimed to bring the translations ever closer into line with the underlying text of the original. The end results of this process of revision were highly sophisticated mirror translations.

But even the translator who sets out to provide such a mirror rendering cannot avoid being interpretative in places; quite frequently (and especially in the Hebrew Old Testament) the original text is ambiguous or obscure, and so the translator is forced to make a choice between two or more possibilities. At Creation (Gen 1:2) is it "the Spirit of God" or a "mighty wind" over the primordial deep? Both ancient and modern translators are divided over this and many other such ambiguities. Indeed, sometimes the very choice of a literal rendering might be considered interpretative: a good example is provided by the first word of the angel Gabriel's greeting to Mary in Luke 1:28; in English the familiar rendering of the Greek "*chaire*" is "hail (Mary)." The standard Syriac biblical text of the New Testament has "*shlam lek(y)*," "Greetings to you," the equivalent Syriac form of the Greek greeting (similarly, the New English Bible has "Greetings"). The very literal seventh-century Syriac version known as the Harclean (Harqloyo) prefers to give instead the etymological equivalent to the Greek, namely the imperative "rejoice." Should the translator pay more attention to the form ("rejoice"), or to the content ("greetings") of the angel's greeting? Ancient translators like the author of the Harclean New Testament thought that the form was more important, while modern translators consider that the content has the greater importance.

We have seen how the invention of printing altered people's attitudes towards the nature of biblical translation. Printing has also had an important effect on the contents of the Bible; this is because printing makes possible the wide circulation of a single edition or translation, resulting in a kind of standardization that was not possible before the invention of printing. We have already seen one such consequence, namely the introduction of a standardized system of chapter and verse numbering. Other kinds of standardization introduced by printing can be seen by comparing the contents and order of books in different modern translations. Bibles produced for the Catholic church will differ from those produced for the various Reformed Churches: the former will contain the "deutero-canonical" books (or "Apocrypha"), while the latter will normally not; and the order of certain Old Testament books will be different. Orthodox Bibles will again differ from both Catholic and Reformed Bibles. Here we can see that the invention of printing has standardized the differences between the various Church traditions.

We should consider one more problem which needs to be faced by the modern biblical translator, since this also has a bearing on our attitude towards the Syriac Bible. What biblical text should the translator treat as authoritative and translate from? At first sight this seems an easy question to answer: the Hebrew text for the Old Testament, and the Greek text for the New Testament. As we shall see, however, this is by no means the only answer. Certainly most modern translations set out to translate from the Hebrew and the Greek, but even here problems arise; the edition of the Hebrew Bible used is in fact a medieval Jewish one where the originally consonantal text has been provided with vowels: it is true that the consonantal text goes back more or less in its present form to the late first century AD, but in many cases (especially in poetic books) this consonantal text can be read with different vowels, providing a somewhat different meaning. Modern translators normally follow the medieval Jewish tradition of understanding the text, but it would also be possible to take the consonantal text as the starting point, without necessarily following the particular interpretation of reading the vowels which the medieval tradition provides. It would also theoretically be possible to take as a starting point an earlier form of the Hebrew text, such as that presupposed by the Septuagint (which in some books must have differed considerably from the Hebrew text we know; in Jeremiah, for example, it was much shorter and had a different order of chapters). Again, someone might reasonably expect a translator to try to go back to the exact form of the Hebrew text as first written down by the individual authors of the Old Testament books. This, however, is an impossible task, for we have no means of getting behind the variety of different forms of the Hebrew text which we now know to have been circulating in the first few centuries BC.

In response to this state of affairs, we need to make use of the distinction between "literary authenticity" and "scriptural authenticity." "Literary authenticity" refers to the exact wording of the original author (which, in the case of the Hebrew Old Testament, is unattainable), whereas "scriptural authenticity" refers to a form of the biblical text which has been held by the religious community as authoritative. This distinction has important consequences: literary authenticity can only apply to a single form of text, but scriptural authenticity can apply simultaneously to several different forms of text. Thus, as far as the Hebrew Bible is concerned, it could be said that scriptural authenticity applies, not only to the medieval Jewish edition of the Hebrew, but also to its consonantal basis which goes back to the late first century, and to the Hebrew text used by the Jewish translators of the Old Testament into Greek. But scriptural authenticity is by no means confined to the Hebrew Old Testament and the Greek New Testament: it applies just as much to the ancient versions, the Greek Septuagint and the Syriac Peshitta, since both these translations have been regarded as authoritative biblical texts by the communities using them.

Once we realize that scriptural authenticity is not necessarily confined to the original biblical languages, it then becomes clear that modern biblical translations should not exclusively be made from Hebrew and Greek: for the Greek and Russian Orthodox Church it would be just as desirable (especially for liturgical use) to use translations from the Septuagint; likewise, in the case of the Churches of Syriac liturgical tradition, it will be important to make available translations from the Syriac Peshitta. These translations would primarily be for use in the liturgy (as we shall see, the Syriac liturgical tradition is rooted in the Syriac Bible); but for other purposes too, they could be profitably used alongside the existing translations from Hebrew and Greek, thus providing an additional source for spiritual insight.

3. A BIRD'S EYE VIEW OF THE SYRIAC BIBLE

For all the Churches of Syriac tradition the authoritative form of the Bible is the Syriac translation known as the Peshitta. The Peshitta Old Testament was translated directly from the original Hebrew text, and the Peshitta New Testament directly from the original Greek. The so-called "deutero-canonical" books, or "Apocrypha," were all translated from Greek, with the exception of Bar Sira (Ecclesiasticus), which was translated from Hebrew.

The date of the Peshitta Old Testament is uncertain, and in any case not all books will have been translated at once, or by the same persons. It is likely that several books will have been inherited by the young Syriac Church from translations made by Jewish communities in the region of Edessa and Nisibis. It seems likely that most books of the Peshitta Old Testament were translated during the period from the second century AD to the early third century AD.

The Peshitta New Testament is in fact a revision of an earlier translation, known as the "Old Syriac." The revision may have been made over a period of time, but was completed sometime in the early fifth century. The circulation of this revision proved extremely effective, for the Peshitta rapidly replaced the Old Syriac and had become the authoritative Syriac text of the New Testament before the schism between the Syrian Orthodox Church and the Church of the East, brought about by the christological controversies of the mid fifth century.

A large number of manuscripts of the Peshitta survive, and the oldest of these date from the fifth and sixth centuries. Since an entire Bible written out by hand was very bulky and awkward to manage, most manuscripts only contain small groups of books at a time and complete Bibles are very rare.

The rarity of complete Bibles before the coming of the printed book has had an important consequence: the precise contents and order of books in the Syriac Bible has never become entirely fixed (even in modern printed editions the order in which the biblical books are printed may differ considerably from one edition to another). As far as contents are concerned, the most important feature of the Syriac Bible is the absence from the original Peshitta translation of the New Testament of some of the Catholic Epistles (2 Peter, 2–3 John, Jude) and the Revelation of St. John (Apocalypse); in most printed editions of the Syriac New Testament, however, the Syriac text of these books has been supplied from later Syriac translations.

Although the Peshitta is the standard biblical text, it is not the only Syriac translation of the Bible.

For the Old Testament, there is a translation made from the Greek Septuagint. This version is known in Syriac as "the Seventy" (*Shab'in*), but is called the "Syro-hexapla" by modern scholars: this was made by the Syrian Orthodox scholar Paul of Tella over the years 614–616 in Alexandria (Egypt). Although the translation was probably never intended for liturgical use, its text is nevertheless sometimes to be found in Syrian Orthodox lectionaries. The Syro-hexapla survives in a number of manuscripts, but unfortunately we do not have the complete text (parts of the Pentateuch and Historical Books are missing).

The Syrian Orthodox scholar Jacob of Edessa (d. 708) made a revised Syriac translation of certain books of the Old Testament, basing his work on both the Greek Septuagint and the Peshitta. Part of his work survives in a small number of very old manuscripts.

A few other relics of translations of individual Old Testament books from Greek into Syriac also survive; these may have been commissioned by the Syrian Orthodox theologian Philoxenus (Aksenoyo) of Mabbug (d. 523).

For the New Testament we know of a number of other Syriac versions, besides the Peshitta:

The oldest Syriac translation of the Gospels was almost certainly in the form of a harmony of the four Gospels known as the Diatessaron, a Greek word meaning "through four," that is, a single Gospel text derived from the four Gospels. Only quotations of the original form of this survive, and much uncertainty surrounds its authorship and origin. The Diatessaron is usually thought to have been composed by Tatian, a native of Mesopotamia who studied in Rome under Justin Martyr in the middle of the second century AD, and then returned to his homeland. It is not known for certain whether he composed his Gospel harmony in Greek or in Syriac. In the early Syriac Church, before the birth of the Peshitta New Testament, the Diatessaron was evidently considered as an authoritative Gospel text, for St. Ephrem wrote a commentary on it in the fourth century. Once the Peshitta New Testament had come in to existence, early in the fifth century, the

Diatessaron fell out of favour, and as result no complete manuscript of it in Syriac survives.

Next in time after the Diatessaron comes the translation known as the "Old Syriac" of which only the Four Gospels survive (preserved in two very early manuscripts). The date when this translation was made remains uncertain; some scholars suggest the late second or early third century, while others prefer the early fourth century. In any case the Old Syriac seems to be later than the Diatessaron and in many places it has been influenced by the Diatessaron. It is likely that the Old Syriac originally extended to the Acts of the Apostles and the Epistles, but no manuscript containing the Old Syriac version of these books survives.

We have already seen that the Peshitta New Testament is in fact not a completely new translation from Greek, but a revision of the Old Syriac, correcting it against the Greek text. Over the period from the fifth to the seventh century Greek language and culture became more and more prestigious in the eyes of Syriac biblical scholars, especially in the Syrian Orthodox Church; as a result, two further revisions of the Syriac New Testament were made, trying to bring it closer into line with the Greek original.

We know that the chorepiscopus Polycarp completed a revision of the Peshitta New Testament in 508. This work had been commissioned by the Syrian Orthodox theologian Philoxenus, metropolitan of Mabbug (Menbij), and so is normally called the "Philoxenian" New Testament. The Philoxenian version is unfortunately lost apart from some quotations: it was evidently never circulated widely and no manuscripts of it survive; it is possible, however, that the surviving sixth-century translations of the Minor Catholic Epistles and Revelation may belong to this revision, in which case we do have the Philoxenian version for a few books, a least.

This lost Philoxenian revision served as the basis for yet a further revision of the Syriac New Testament, completed in 616 in Alexandria by the Syrian Orthodox Scholar Thomas of Harkel. This revision, known as the "Harclean" (Harqloyo), provides a remarkable mirror translation, reflecting every detail of the Greek original. The Harklean was widely circulated in Syrian Orthodox circles and was often used for Gospel lectionaries. The Harklean New Testament survives complete, and includes the Minor Catholic Epistles and Revelation.

Thus for the Syriac Bible we have, in tabular form:

OLD TESTAMENT   Hebrew   → Peshitta
                                (c. 2nd cent. AD)
                  Greek   → Philoxenian
                                (Isaiah; early 6th cent.)
                  Greek   → Syro-hexapla
                  (Septuagint)   (616)
                  Greek and   → revision by Jacob of Edessa
                  Peshitta   (certain books only; c.700)

NEW TESTAMENT   Greek   → Diatessaron
                                (Gospel Harmony, 2nd cent. AD)
                              → Old Syriac
                                (c. 3rd cent.)
                              → Peshitta
                                (c. 400)
                              → Philoxenian
                                (508)
                              → Harklean
                                (616)

CHAPTER II
THE SYRIAC BIBLE - A CLOSER LOOK

1. OLD TESTAMENT

TRANSLATED FROM HEBREW: "PESHITTA"

The name "Peshitta" means "straightforward, simple"; it was given to the standard Syriac versions of the Bible (both Old and New Testaments) in order to distinguish them from the seventh-century translations, the Syro-hexapla and the Harclean. The name is first encountered in the ninth-century writer Mushe bar Kipho; earlier authors had simply referred to the Peshitta as "the Syriac."

The origins of the Peshitta translation are very obscure and Syriac authors had no clear memory of how and when the work was carried out (a few implausible guesses were nevertheless circulated). A close study of the translation itself can throw a little light; from such a study we can deduce the following:

The Peshitta Old Testament is not the work of a single translator, but must have been carried out by many different translators, perhaps working over a considerable period of time.

The translators all worked basically from the Hebrew text, and this Hebrew text was essentially the same as the consonantal Hebrew text of our printed Hebrew Bibles. Since we know that this consonantal text became the authoritative Hebrew text some time in the late first century AD, it is likely that the translators were working after it had been widely propagated.

In some books the translators seem to have consulted or made use of other translations: thus at various places in the Pentateuch (Genesis, Deuteronomy) there are some remarkable links between the Peshitta and the Jewish Aramaic Targums and for some of the Prophets and Wisdom books the translators probably consulted the Septuagint on occasion, in order to seek help over difficult passages in Hebrew. The links with the Targums in certain books leads us to suppose that at least for these books the translators were probably Jewish, rather than Christian. In other books, however, the evidence perhaps points to Christian translators, though it is likely that such people were of Jewish origin, for a knowledge of Hebrew would otherwise be difficult to explain.

For the student of Bible translations it is of particular interest to look at the distinctive features of a translation. Here we shall concentrate on some unusual interpretative renderings to be found in different books of the Peshitta Old Testament; many of these have their roots in Jewish exegetical tradition.

It was pointed out in Chapter I that even the translator who sets out to provide a literal translation cannot avoid choosing between two or more possible interpretations in cases where the Hebrew original is obscure or ambiguous. The Hebrew text of God's words to Cain in Genesis 4:7, "if you do well, will you not be accepted" (Revised Standard Version), is capable of several possible interpretations, owing to the ambiguity of the word *s't* ("will you not be accepted?" in the RSV). *S't* derives from the verb *nasa* which can have at least four different senses, all possible in the context:

(1) "raise up" in the sense of "offer." This is how the Greek Septuagint takes it ("If you offer well…").

(2) "lift up" in the sense of "accept." The Syriac translator opts for this understanding, and he gives emphasis to it by changing the tense: he translates using a past tense, *qabblet*, literally "I have received/ accepted," but in this context it will either have the nuance "I will certainly accept (that is, if you (= Cain) act well in future), or "I would have accepted" (that is, if you had acted well on the first occasion). Two Jewish Greek revisers of the Greek Bible have a similar understanding of the word.

(3) "lift up" in the sense of "forgive." This is how the Jewish Targums understand the passage ("you will be forgiven").

(4) "lift up" in the sense of "suspend." This understanding of the word was chosen by the author of the Samaritan Targum ("I will suspend"). It is interesting to find that most modern translators base their renderings on the second interpretation, thus following in the footsteps of the Peshitta.

In the next verse (4:8) the Hebrew has evidently lost some words, for it reads "And Cain said to his brother (…). And when they were in the field Cain rose up against his brother Abel and killed him." All the ancient versions, including the Peshitta, supply some appropriate words, usually "Let us go out into the field." But the Peshitta translator does something else as well: instead of translating the Hebrew word "field" literally, he renders it by "valley" (*pqaʿta*). What is the reason for this seemingly willful alteration? A clue to the answer is to be found in Ezekiel , where Paradise is described as a mountain. There is no hint of this in the Hebrew text of

Genesis, but Jewish and Christian readers regularly understood the topography of Genesis 1–4 in the light of Ezekiel (the idea was also popularized in the non-canonical book known as Enoch): Paradise was understood as a mountain, and when Adam and Eve were driven out of Paradise they took up residence on the foothills at the mountain's base. Abel and Cain made their sacrifice on one of these foothills, but when Cain took Abel off with the intention of killing him, he took him down on to lower ground, in other words, the "valley" which the Peshitta translator has actually introduced into the biblical text here. Early commentaries on the passage often understand the topography in this way, but the Peshitta is the only biblical translation which incorporates this understanding into the Bible itself.

According to the Hebrew text of Genesis 8:5 Noah's Ark landed on mount Ararat (in Armenia, modern northeast Turkey), and "Ararat" will be found in all modern translations. In the Peshitta, however, the Ark rests on "the mountains of Qardu," that is to say, considerably further south, in Kurdistan (modern southeast Turkey). This was not, of course, a willful rendering on the part of the translator: here, as in many other places, he is simply following Jewish tradition which was current in his day. "Ararat" of the Hebrew text was identified as Qardu both by Josephus, writing in Greek in the later first century AD, and by the Jewish Aramaic translations of the Bible, known as the Targums. Thanks to this identification in the Peshitta, Mount Qardu has been a place for local pilgrimage even into modern times.

Genesis 22, on Abraham's sacrifice of Isaac, is a chapter to which we shall return later, in Chapter IV. The Peshitta translation of the chapter already has a number of distinctive features. The two most prominent ones are in verses 2 and 12. Verse two provides the location where the sacrifice is to take place: the Hebrew text has "the land of Moriah," which allowed later tradition to identify the place as the site of the Temple, since the only other occurrence of Moriah in the Hebrew Bible is at 2 Chronicles 3:1, which tells how "Solomon began to build the House of the Lord in Jerusalem on Mount Moriah, where the Lord had appeared to David his father." Modern translations follow the Hebrew text in speaking of Moriah in both passages, but the ancient translators knew of some quite different traditions: the Greek Septuagint has "high land" in Genesis and "mountain of the Amorites" in Chronicles, while the Syriac Peshitta has "land of the Amorites" in Genesis, and "mountain of the Amorites" in Chronicles. The Latin translation known as the Vulgate knows yet another exegetical tradition, and in Genesis it has "land of vision," an etymological rendering of Moriah, linking it with the Hebrew verb *ra'ah*, "to see"; Jerome derived

this rendering from the earlier Jewish Greek revision of the Hebrew Bible
by Symmachus.

The second distinctive feature of Genesis 22 in the Peshitta occurs in
verse 12, where in the Hebrew (followed by the Septuagint and by all
modern translations) the angel says "for now I know that you fear God."
By contrast the Peshitta reads "for now I have made known that you fear
God" (the text was often later read as "for now you have made known that
you fear God," since the consonantal text 'wd't can be read either as awd'et,
"I have made known," or as awda't, "you have made known"). This might
not seem a very important difference, but in fact it implies a very different
setting for this fearsome trial of Abraham: God allows the trial to take
place, not to find out himself whether Abraham's love for God and his faith
were stronger than his love for Isaac his son; rather, God allows it to take
place because some of the angels doubt whether Abraham is worthy of the
special title given him of "Friend of God." The setting for the trial of
Abraham is thus understood as being very similar to the setting for the trials
of Job, which were initiated because Satan, the "Adversary," likewise
doubted the strength of Job's faith. This understanding of the background
to Genesis 22 is explicitly found in early Jewish exegetical tradition; the
Peshitta, however, is the only ancient translation to have introduced a hint
of this interpretation into the actual biblical text.

The Peshitta translation of Genesis, and indeed of the Pentateuch as a
whole, is particularly rich in links with contemporary Jewish exegetical
tradition, and this makes it likely that these books were translated by Jews
rather than by Christians.

Another place where the Peshitta translation has a great many
distinctive renderings, often Jewish in character, is the two books of
Chronicles. Here, for example, a number of the place names have been
"updated" and identified with places in northern Mesopotamia which will
have been more familiar to Syriac readers; thus, for example, Aram Ma'acah
(1 Chr 19:6) is identified as Harran, and Carcemish (2 Chr 35:20) with
Mabbug. Quite often the Syriac translator uses phraseology which is typical
of the Jewish Targums (though there are very few links with the surviving
Targum to Chronicles, which is probably later in date than the Peshitta).
Thus at 2 Chronicles 1:7 where the Hebrew has "In that night God
appeared to Solomon (and said to him, 'Ask what I shall give you'," the
Syriac has "In that night the Lord was revealed over Solomon." The
wording "was revealed over" is characteristic of the Jewish Palestinian
Targum tradition (and is occasionally also found in the Peshitta
Pentateuch), in contrast to the Babylonian Targum's regular use of "was

revealed to." Another case where the Peshitta employs wording which is distinctively Jewish in character is to be found in passages like 2 Chronicles 33:7, where God speaks of his presence in the Temple; in that particular passage the Hebrew has "In this House and in Jerusalem ... I will put my name for ever," but in the Syriac the last phrase appears as "I will cause my Shekhina (the divine presence) to reside for ever." Such phraseology is characteristic of the Jewish Targums, and is not to be found in any of the other ancient translations of the Bible.

One other book in the Peshitta has close links with the Targum, namely Proverbs. Here the situation is unique, for the Peshitta and the Targum are virtually word for word the same much of the time, and one must definitely derive from the other. One would expect the Peshitta to be derived from the Targum, but on linguistic grounds it can be shown that in fact the Targum must derive in this book from the Peshitta. This means that the Peshitta translation of Proverbs is also likely to have been the work of Jews in northern Mesopotamia: it subsequently came to be taken over by Syriac-speaking Christians and by later Jews (who lightly modified the dialect).

In other books of the Peshitta Old Testament the links with the Targums are much more tenuous, or altogether absent. In these other books the translators have introduced much fewer interpretative elements, and their rendering is usually rather close to the Hebrew, though in some books they occasionally make use of the Septuagint in isolated passages.

TRANSLATED FROM GREEK: SYRO-HEXAPLA

Over the course of the fifth to seventh centuries AD Christian literature in Greek came to have great prestige in the eyes of the Syriac churches. This was due to a number of different reasons, but the most important of these was the fact that Greek was the main cultural language of the eastern Roman Empire and so the theological controversies of the fifth and following centuries were conducted primarily in Greek. Since Syriac readers were anxious to be brought up to date in theological developments, huge numbers of theological works were translated from Greek into Syriac, and by the end of the seventh century almost all the main Greek Fathers had been translated into Syriac, either in whole or in part. As time went on, translators tried to represent the Greek more and more exactly in Syriac, and by the seventh century they had developed very sophisticated methods of "mirror-translation," aimed at reflecting all the details of the Greek original in the Syriac translation.

It is against this general background of translation activity that we should look at the seventh-century Syriac biblical translations, the Syro-hexapla for the Old Testament, and the Harclean for the New.

The Syro-hexapla was primarily the work of Paul, bishop of Tella, a scholar working at the monastery of the Antonines at the Ennaton (or ninth milestone), just outside the great city of Alexandria in Egypt. We know that he was engaged in the arduous task over the period 615–617, and these dates explain why he was not looking after his flock in Tella (in northern Mesopotamia): in 614 the Persians had invaded the Roman Empire and seized, not only northern Syria and Mesopotamia, but also the holy city of Jerusalem. Only shortly after Paul completed his work they also took Alexandria, and it is fortunate that his translation was not lost then. Paul was thus a refugee, and it is worth remembering that this great work of scholarship was undertaken at a time of great political turmoil and uncertainty.

It seems that the translation was commissioned by the Syrian Orthodox patriarch Athanasius. Instead of using the ordinary text of the Septuagint, Paul worked from Origen's revision of the Septuagint, bringing it into closer line with the Hebrew original. Origen's revision, undertaken in the early third century, was incorporated into a massive six-columned Bible known as the Hexapla ("Six-fold"), which probably contained: the Hebrew text, first in Hebrew characters and then in Greek transcription; two Jewish Greek translations (Aquila and Symmachus); Origen's own revision of the Septuagint; and another Jewish Greek translation, by Theodotion. Paul translated the fifth column, containing the revised Septuagint text, but in the margins he sometimes included information taken from the other columns; it is for this reason that his translation is known today as the Syro-hexapla (Syriac writers themselves refer to it under another name, "the Seventy," that is, based on the Septuagint). Paul's translation reflects the Greek very closely, and this has proved most useful for modern scholars, seeing that Origen's Hexapla has been lost, apart from a few fragments. (As we shall see below, in Chapter III, Paul's own translation does not survive complete).

The Syro-hexapla enjoyed considerable popularity in the Syrian Orthodox Church, and sometimes its text, rather than the Peshitta's, was used in Old Testament Lectionaries. Although Timothy I, the patriarch of the Church of the East, showed an interest in having a manuscript of the Syro-hexapla copied at the beginning of the eighth century, this version was never used in the Lectionaries of the Church of the East; it is, however, quite often referred to in several of the commentaries of the ninth century (see Chapter V).

It is important to realize that the Syro-hexapla was not the only source of knowledge of the Septuagint's biblical text for Syriac readers. In the sixth century there were translations of some individual books of the Old Testament made from Greek (fragments of a version of Isaiah survive), and it is possible that these were commissioned by Philoxenus, bishop of Mabbug. Then in his old age, in the early years of eighth century, the great Syrian Orthodox scholar Jacob of Edessa undertook another translation from Greek, but also keeping some elements from the Peshitta. His work evidently covered several books of the Old Testament, but only a few survive today (Pentateuch, 1–2 Samuel, I Kings, Isaiah, Ezekiel, and Daniel; some of these only in fragmentary form).

There was one further important source of knowledge of the Septuagint's biblical text: this was not in the form of an actual biblical translation, but was available indirectly, in translations of the Greek Fathers into Syriac. These Greek writers of course quoted the Old Testament from the Septuagint, and when their works were translated into Syriac the practice of the Syriac translators from about AD 500 onwards was to translate the biblical quotations from the Septuagint exactly as they found them (earlier they had often adapted the quotations to the Peshitta text, since that was the biblical text which was familiar to their readers). It was through these translations of Greek patristic texts that many exegetical traditions based on the Septuagint, rather than on the Peshitta, reached the Syriac Churches: we shall later on look at passages where the differences between the Greek and the Syriac caused some intriguing problems which have left their mark in some liturgical texts (Chapter VII, on Gen 1:2).

2. NEW TESTAMENT

DIATESSARON

The harmony of the four Gospels known as the Diatessaron is associated with Tatian, an important Syrian theologian who wrote in Greek just after the middle of the second century. Tatian had studied in Rome under Justin Martyr before returning to the East (his exact home is unknown). It is uncertain when, where, and in what language he composed the Diatessaron: the original work is unfortunately lost, but traces of it can be found in the Christian West as well as in the Christian East. As far as the Syriac Churches are concerned, it is certain that the Diatessaron circulated widely in Syriac and that it was regarded as an authoritative form of the Gospel text until the early fifth century, when it was suppressed in favor of the separate four Gospels. In the fourth century St. Ephrem even wrote a commentary on the Diatessaron, and it is this work which is our most important witness to the actual text of the Diatessaron.

At the time when Tatian was compiling the Diatessaron the idea of a canonical set of four Gospels was only in its infancy. This explains why he felt able to take certain liberties with the text, even introducing here and there features which are not to be found in the four Gospels of Matthew, Mark, Luke, and John. The following are three examples of such features.

In Matthew 4:4 and Mark 1:6 John the Baptist is said to have lived off "locusts and wild honey." Many later readers were surprised that an ascetic like John should have eaten a non-vegetarian diet, with locusts, and various interpretations were put forward suggesting that the Greek word in question in fact meant some sort of plant. Tatian evidently took a more radical course, removing the offending word used by Matthew and Mark altogether, and subsisting "milk of the mountains"; John the Baptist, according to this new reading, lived off milk and honey, in other words, the food of the Promised Land (Deuteronomy 6:3). The Old Testament association was certainly intentional on Tatian's part, for the entry into the Promised Land was seen as a typological counterpart to Christian baptism.

31

In the account of Jesus' baptism in the Jordan (Matt 3:16, Mark 1:10, Luke 3:22) Tatian introduced a detail which is absent from the three Gospels: as Jesus entered the water "a great light appeared." This was certainly not an entirely new invention on Tatian's part; rather, he was simply adapting a tradition already in existence that fire had appeared at Jesus' baptism. In Tatian's theology (which we know of from his Oration to the Greeks) light is a much more important theological symbol than fire, and it is probably for this reason that he made the alteration (only one letter's difference in Syriac: *nura* "fire," but *nuhra* "light").

The familiar text of Jesus' words to Peter in Matthew 16:18 reads "on this rock will I build my church, and the gates of hell shall not prevail against it." Here the precise meaning of "gates of hell" is far from clear; most modern translations take it as a metaphor and render it by "powers of death" (thus e.g., Revised Standard Version, New English Bible). The Syriac Diatessaron had a rather different wording, employing "bars of Sheol" instead (Sheol is the Hebrew and Aramaic term for the place of the dead). At first sight this leaves the passage just as obscure, but if we realize that the mention of "bars" carries with it an allusion to two Old Testament passages, Psalm 107:16 and Isaiah 45:2, then the intention behind the alteration becomes clear: these passages, where God is described as "shattering the doors of bronze and breaking the bars of iron," were interpreted in the early Church as referring to Christ's descent into Sheol. By introducing the allusion to these Old Testament passages which were taken as prefiguring Christ's descent into Sheol, Tatian is providing the reader with a clue how to interpret Matthew 16:18: Christ is promising Peter that the bars and gates of Sheol will not be able to prevail against the Church just as they would not be able to prevail against him at his coming descent into Sheol; just as he would shatter the doors and break the bars of Sheol as he rose from the dead, so too would the Church at the final resurrection.

In two of these changes to the wording of the text Tatian has introduced allusions to the Old Testament. This is in itself of interest, for he was writing at a time when Marcion and his followers were throwing out the Old Testament from use in the Church.

The first and third of these alterations are known solely from Syriac and other eastern witnesses, and they have left no trace in the western Diatessaron witnesses, such as the medieval vernacular Gospel harmonies. Thus there is the possibility that they are the work of the author of the Syriac Diatessaron, rather than of Tatian (supposing that he wrote the Diatessaron in Greek, rather than Syriac).

OLD SYRIAC

The Old Syriac version of the New Testament is known to us only from two ancient manuscripts, both containing just the Gospels. There must have been a Syriac translation of Acts and the Epistles prior to the time of the Peshitta revision (ca. 400), since Ephrem (d. 373) comments on these books; very little, however, can be recovered of the actual wording of that part of the Old Syriac. In what follows the term Old Syriac will refer only to the Old Syriac translation of the Gospels.

The two manuscripts containing the Old Syriac Gospel are today known as the Curetonian (C: after William Cureton, its first editor) and the Sinaitic (S; since the manuscript belongs to St. Catherine's Monastery in Sinai). Neither is complete, and the Sinaitic manuscript is often illegible since the original text has been sponged off and another quite different text has then been superimposed. Both C and S have the title "Gospel of the separated (Evangelists)," *Evangelion da-Mepharreshe*, which is evidently meant to distinguish this version of the four separate Gospels from the "Gospel of the Mingled (Evangelists)," *Evangelion da-Mehallete*, which refers to the Diatessaron.

The date when the Old Syriac translation was made is very uncertain, though it is now thought probably that it is later than the Diatessaron. The dates to which modern scholars have assigned the translation range from the late second century to the early fourth century (the two manuscripts themselves probably both belong to the fifth century).

The text of the Old Syriac quite often differs considerably from the Peshitta, and this is for two main reasons: (1) the Old Syriac translation was made from a Greek text which differed in many respects from the Greek text underlying the Peshitta revision, and (2) the style of translation is much more free (at least in many places). It is interesting that the translator clearly felt that the Syriac Old Testament (Peshitta) had greater authority for his readers than the Greek New Testament, for he adapts Old Testament quotations in the Gospels to the wording of the Peshitta Old Testament in a number of cases where this differs from the form of the quotation found in the Greek New Testament. This is in fact a practice adopted by many early Syriac translators of Greek Patristic writings, and it is only from about AD 500 that translators change their attitude and prefer to translate biblical quotations in the form in which they find them in their Greek text, even when this may go against the wording of the Peshitta Bible.

The text of the two manuscripts is by no means identical, though they have enough in common to indicate that they are both witnesses to the same translation. Probably both manuscripts have a text which has been revised, or corrected against the Greek here and there. This would explain, for example, why S has the shorter ending of Mark (ending at 16:8), while C has the longer ending (concluding at 16:20).

As one might expect in the earliest surviving Syriac text of the Gospels, the Old Syriac contains a number of archaisms in grammar and vocabulary. Sometimes these have been taken to reflect Palestinian Aramaic forms (with the implication that the translators were either of Palestinian origin themselves, or possibly had access to oral traditions in Palestinian Aramaic): this suggestion rests on a misunderstanding, for the archaisms are best explained as survivals from an earlier stage in the history of Syriac itself.

PESHITTA

The standard form of the Syriac New Testament, the Peshitta, is not a new translation from Greek, but a revision of the Old Syriac, bringing it into closer line with the Greek. As we have seen, the two Old Syriac manuscripts C and S themselves show traces of sporadic revision. It seems likely that the process of revision which resulted in the Peshitta text as we know it was a long one, reaching its completion in the early fifth century. In its final form the revision seems to have been "marketed" very successfully, for it evidently rapidly replaced the Old Syriac and Diatessaron and became the standard text for all the Syriac Churches. Traces of the older versions, the Diatessaron and Old Syriac, did nevertheless survive here and there, both as isolated readings in a few Peshitta manuscripts, and in quotations by later writers; thus, for example, the reading of the Syriac Diatessaron at Matthew 16:18, "bars of Sheol" (as opposed to "gates of Sheol" in both the Old Syriac and the Peshitta), is still known to many writers after the fifth century, long after the Diatessaron itself had been officially suppressed.

It has been suggested that the Peshitta revision was actually the work of the great bishop of Edessa, Rabbula (who died in 435). This, however, now seems unlikely, though Edessa (with its famous theological school) may have been the place from which the final form of the revision was propagated. It is interesting that many early Peshitta manuscripts contain the "Eusebian canons," which provide a convenient system of cross references between the different Gospels (each Gospel is divided into numbered sections): perhaps this was a specific feature which accompanied the new "edition" of the Syriac New Testament.

The Peshitta covers only those books which were regarded by the Syriac Church as authoritative, namely, the Gospels, Acts, the Pauline Epistles, James, I Peter, and I John. In early Peshitta manuscripts the

Catholic Epistles come between Acts and the Pauline Epistles, and not after the latter. 2 Peter, 2–3 John, Jude, and Revelation were not translated into Syriac until the sixth century (possibly as part of the Philoxenian version, though this is not at all certain). A number of isolated verses, familiar from English translations of the New Testament, are also missing from the Peshitta: Matthew 27:35b, Luke 22:17–18, John 7:53–8:11 (the woman caught in adultery), Acts 8:37, 15:34, and 28:29; in modern printed editions these are usually supplied from some later version.

There is remarkably little variation between different manuscripts of the Peshitta New Testament: only a rather small number of Peshitta manuscripts preserve a few isolated readings which go back to the Old Syriac. There are, however, one or two passages of theological interest where variation has crept in. The most famous of such passages is the end of Hebrews 2:9, where manuscripts of East Syriac provenance regularly have "for he (Jesus), apart from God, tasted death on behalf of everyone" while manuscripts of West Syriac origin have "for, by grace, God tasted death on behalf of everyone." The variation has its origin in the Greek: there the majority of manuscripts have "by the grace of God" (*chariti theou*), but a very small number have "without God" (*choris theou*). Scholars have long argued over which of these is the original reading, but as far as the Peshitta is concerned it would seem that "by grace God" (slightly different from the Greek's "by the grace of God") may belong to the original Syriac translation, while "without God" was perhaps introduced into East Syriac manuscripts at an early date under the influence of Theodore of Mopsuestia's strong support for that reading (which for him had the advantage of avoiding any idea of the Godhead suffering at the crucifixion: it is only the Man who tasted death, not God the Word).

PHILOXENIAN

There has been much confusion among scholars over the relationship between the Philoxenian and the Harclean versions of the Syriac New Testament, but some recently published commentaries on the Gospels by Philoxenus himself have provided a definite solution. Thus we now know that the Philoxenian version is lost, and that the very literal translation which does survive is the Harclean (despite the fact that its first editor unfortunately gave it the title "versio Philoxeniana").

The Philoxenian New Testament was not a completely new translation, but a revision of the Peshitta, commissioned by Philoxenus of Mabbug and carried out by his chorepiscopos Polycarp. The work was completed in 507/8. Although no manuscripts containing the Philoxenian survive, a number of quotations from it are preserved in Philoxenus' Commentaries on the Gospels: furthermore, in one of these (the Commentary on the Prologue of John) Philoxenus explains why he commissioned the revision. Philoxenus, who lived at a time of heated theological controversy, was unhappy with some rather free renderings in the Peshitta of passages such as Matthew 1:1, 1:18, and Hebrews 5:7 and 10:5, all of which have important theological implications for a proper understanding of the nature of the incarnation. Philoxenus complained that the rather loose rendering of these verses in the Peshitta gave possible scope for "a Nestorian interpretation" (as he called it); accordingly he saw the need for a more exact rendering of the Greek New Testament into Syriac. He himself put it as follows:

> When those of old undertook to translate these passages they made mistakes in many things, whether intentionally or through ignorance. These mistakes concerned not only what is taught about the Economy in the flesh, but various other things concerning different matters. It was for this reason that we have now taken the trouble to have the Holy Scriptures translated anew from Greek into Syriac.

Philoxenus' comments on Hebrews 5:7 illustrate the sort of wording he was concerned about. First of all he quotes what he considers to be the correct translation of the Greek, "He, who in the days of his flesh....."; he then goes on as follows:

> In place of this they (the Peshitta's translators) translated "when he was clothed in the flesh," and instead of translating Paul they inclined towards the position of Nestorius, who cast the body onto the Word as one does a garment onto an ordinary body, or as purple is put on emperors (these are both favorite analogies among East Syriac writers).

From these and other remarks by Philoxenus himself, we can see that the prime motivation behind the Philoxenian New Testament was provided by the theological controversies of the time and the need for an accurate and literal translation of the Greek New Testament.

It is possible that the anonymous sixth-century translation of the minor Catholic Epistles (2 Peter, 2–3 John, Jude) and Revelation may belong to the Philoxenian New Testament, in which cases they would be the only surviving representatives of this version. The style of translation would seem appropriate for what we know of the Philoxenian, but against this we need to weigh the fact that Philoxenus himself never seems to quote from these books, which would be a little surprising if he was the person who had commissioned their first translation into Syriac.

HARCLEAN

The Harclean version represents the culmination of the long process of revision of the Syriac translation of the New Testament. Its author was Thomas of Harkel, who worked at the same monastery as Paul of Tella, outside Alexandria, and at the same time; he completed his work in 616. Their technique of highly sophisticated literal translation is very similar.

Thomas worked on the basis of the previous revision, the Philoxenian, and he covered the entire New Testament, including the minor Catholic Epistles and Revelation. In contrast to the Philoxenian, where the motivation seems to have been primarily theological, the Harclean displays a much greater interest in philological detail: every particle of the Greek original is reflected in the translation. Thomas regularly strives to achieve a formal equivalence between the Greek and the Syriac text, with the result that it is possible for the modern scholar to reconstruct the Greek text which he must have used as the basis for his revision. As a matter of fact, Thomas did not confine himself to one Greek manuscript, for the colophon, or note at the end of the text, in many Harclean manuscripts speaks of his having used two or three different Greek manuscripts. It so happens that one of the Greek manuscripts which he used in Acts is of great interest for the study of the transmission of the Greek text of the New Testament, since it contains an archaic type of the textual tradition which is not well attested elsewhere.

The Harclean version soon became popular in the Syrian Orthodox Church and it was often used in Lectionary manuscripts, instead of the Peshitta. It was also used as the basis for a harmony of the four Gospels which covered the Passion narrative.

CHAPTER III
HOW DOES THE SYRIAC BIBLE REACH US?

In this section we shall look at the ways in which the Syriac Bible is transmitted to us. Needless to say, no autographs of any of the original translators survive; in the case of the Syro-hexapla and Harclean, however, we do have some manuscripts which must have been written less than a century after these translations had been made.

1. BIBLICAL MANUSCRIPTS

A very large number of Syriac biblical manuscripts survive. These are always in codex or book format, and the writing material used is either vellum or paper (which was introduced in the Middle Ages). The manuscripts can vary in size, from the enormous "pandects" containing the whole Old Testament or whole New Testament (very rarely both together), to miniature manuscripts written in a tiny script containing a single book or small groups of books. The vast majority of manuscripts, however, are of more practical sizes, and normally they contain just a group of books at a time. Occasionally one may find a biblical book incorporated into a manuscript which otherwise contains non-biblical texts.

Many manuscripts have a colophon, or note by the scribe, at the end, and this may give information about the place where the manuscript was written, and the date. Normally the date is given according to the Seleucid era, or "reckoning of the Greeks," or "of Alexander (the Great)," which began in October, BC 312: thus, for example, the year 771 of the Seleucid era will correspond to October 459 to September 460 in the Christian era.

The oldest dated Syriac biblical manuscript, a fragment of Isaiah in the British Library (Add. 14512), is in fact dated to 771 "according to the Greeks," that is, AD 459/60; another manuscript also in London (Add. 14425), containing Genesis and Exodus, is dated 463/4. For the Peshitta New Testament the earliest dated manuscript is a Gospel manuscript written in Edessa in 510; there are, however, some undated ones which probably belong to the fifth century.

A few manuscripts contain more than one different biblical version at the same time, arranged in parallel columns. Thus there is one fragmentary manuscript containing the Peshitta and Syro-hexapla of Isaiah set side by side. More frequently such manuscripts are genuinely polyglot, and have versions in different languages. One of the earliest polyglot manuscripts is a ninth-century Psalter, now in St. Petersburg; this has the Greek, the Syro-hexapla, and the Arabic texts set out in three columns. More ambitious in scope are a group of fourteenth-century manuscripts evidently written in Egypt, for the most part intended for liturgical use among the multi-lingual groups of monks in the Nitrian Desert. Two of these are Psalters which anticipate the earliest European polyglot Psalter of 1516; one of them has the text set out in five columns, containing Ethiopic, Syriac (Peshitta), Coptic, Arabic, and Armenian; the other has the text in four columns, and this time the languages are Arabic, Syriac (Syro-hexapla), Greek, and Hebrew. The inclusion of Hebrew in a Christian biblical manuscript at that time seems to be without parallel, and clearly the monk who compiled the manuscript must have been a remarkable scholar for his time.

As far as each individual Syriac version is concerned, we have the following picture:

Old Testament (1) Peshitta

There are very few manuscripts containing the complete Old Testament; it is significant that the majority of these belong to the seventeenth century, for by that time the invention of printing had accustomed people to the idea of a complete Old Testament, or a complete Bible: these manuscripts were in fact written only shortly before the first printed edition of the whole Syriac Bible (the Paris Polyglot, of 1645; see below, on EDITIONS). The four earliest manuscripts containing (or once containing) the complete Peshitta Bible (Old and New Testaments) are:

- The codex Ambrosianus, in the Ambrosian Library, Milan, Italy (ms B. 21 Inf; 7a1 in the Leiden edition of the Peshitta Old Testament); this is written in a beautiful Estrangelo script which can be dated to the sixth or seventh century.

- Paris, Bibliothèque Nationale, Syriac ms 341 (8a1 in the Leiden edition); this is written in a neat Estrangelo belonging to the eighth century, and it contains some illustrations (portraits of Old Testament figures, and some scenes).

- Florence, Laurentian Library, ms Or. 58 (9a1 in the Leiden edition) this: is written in Serto script which can be dated to the ninth century.

- Cambridge, University Library, ms Oo. I. 1,2 (12a1 in the Leiden edition); this is written in a neat Estrangelo script which can be dated to the twelfth century; it also contains some illustrations in the form of small portraits of biblical persons. This manuscript has important connections with India, for it was once in Kerala. Although it was written in northern Mesopotamia, the manuscript was taken to India, perhaps some time in the eighteenth century, for in 1806 the Syrian Orthodox bishop Mar Dionysius I (Mar

Thomas VI) presented it to Dr. Claudius Buchanan, Vice-Principal of Fort William College Calcutta. Dr. Buchanan had spoken to him of plans of printing the Syriac Bible in England, and this was the reason for Mar Dionysius' generous gift. Use was indeed made of "the Buchanan Bible" (as the manuscript came to be called) in preparing the printed edition, and when it was finally published (in 1823) copies were sent to Kerala. (This edition has recently (1979) been re-issued by the United Bible Societies).

If we compare the contents and order of books in these four complete Old Testaments, we will discover that they all differ in several respects both in the books they contain and in the order in which they give them. It is thus clear that neither contents nor order of books was regarded as being at all fixed. This is in fact hardly surprising when one remembers that manuscripts containing the complete Bible are the exception, and that normally a biblical manuscript will only contain a group of books (such as the Pentateuch) at a time.

The order of books in the oldest of these complete Peshitta Bibles, the codex Ambrosianus, has a number of interesting features which are worth looking at briefly; the order and contents are as follows: Pentateuch, Job, Joshua, Judges, 1–2 Samuel, Psalms, 1–2 Kings, Proverbs, Wisdom of Solomon, Ecclesiastes, Song of Songs, Isaiah, Jeremiah, Lamentations, Letters of Jeremiah and of Baruch, Baruch, Ezekiel, 12 Minor Prophets, Daniel, Bel and the Dragon, Ruth, Susanna, Esther, Judith, Ben Sira, 1–2 Chronicles, Apocalypse of Baruch, IV Ezra (Esdras), Ezra, Nehemiah, 1–4 Maccabees, with a fifth book, which is in fact Book VI of Josephus' *The Jewish War*.

The contents have a number of surprises, for we find included here several books which are considered by most Western churches to be outside the Old Testament Canon, and among these are several which are not even to be found in the so-called "Apocrypha" or Deutero-Canonical Books. This applied above all to the Apocalypse of Baruch and IV Ezra, both of which are long apocalyptic works of Jewish origin and dating probably from the late first century AD; the codex Ambrosianus is in fact the only Syriac manuscript to contain these two books in full (there are some extracts included in a few Lectionaries). Both books were translated into Syriac from Greek but the Greek text does not survive (apart from a few fragments for the Apocalypse of Baruch); for IV Ezra there is also a Latin and a Georgian translation in existence, but for the Apocalypse of

Baruch we have no other witness apart from this manuscript and a later Arabic translation.

The order of the books also has a number of surprises: in the first place, we can observe that the scribe has for the most part tried to arrange them in historical order, according to the date of each book's supposed author. This explains why Psalms (attributed to David) comes between Samuel and Kings; and why the various books attributed to Solomon follow Kings. It also explains why Job follows immediately after the Pentateuch when one realizes Job has been identified with Jobab (Gen 10:29); probably the same tradition was already known by the Essene Community at Qumran, for the only biblical manuscripts from Qumran written in the Old Hebrew script are books of the Pentateuch and Job: evidently this particular script was reserved for books originating in the patriarchal period. This position for Job is in fact quite common in Syriac biblical manuscripts (thus it likewise follows the Pentateuch in both the Paris and the Cambridge complete Peshitta Bibles).

It will be noticed that codex Ambrosianus groups all the books on women together (Ruth, Susanna, Esther, Judith). This seems to have been quite a widespread practice from the sixth century onwards, and this group of books is often given the title "the Book of the Women."

It is of interest to have some idea of the number of manuscripts containing parts of the Peshitta Old Testament. In the following list, arranged by century, it is important to remember that (1) the dating of Syriac manuscripts is often rather uncertain (only a few biblical manuscripts have dates provided in the colophons); and (2) the great majority of these manuscripts contain only a single group of books at a time (or sometimes only one book).

Sixth cent.	27mss (often only one book, and often fragmentary)
Seventh cent.	32 mss (same applies)
Eight cent.	10 mss
Ninth cent.	12 mss
Tenth cent.	23 mss
Eleventh cent.	5 mss
Twelfth cent.	9 mss
Thirteenth cent.	7 mss
Fourteenth cent.	3 mss
Fifteenth cent.	6 mss
Sixteenth cent.	16 mss
Seventeenth cent.	26 mss

Eighteenth cent. 17 mss
Nineteenth cent. 23 mss

For the rather large number of early manuscripts we owe a special debt of gratitude to the abbot Moses of the Syrian Monastery in the Nitrian Desert (between Cairo and Alexandria in Egypt), for in the early tenth century he collected together a fine library of old Syriac manuscripts which he acquired in Mesopotamia. Subsequently most of the manuscripts in the Syrian Monastery's library came to the Vatican Library (in the eighteenth century) and the British Museum—now Library—(nineteenth century).

The earliest manuscripts are divided up into unnumbered paragraphs. It is intriguing to discover that in some books at least (notably Isaiah), these paragraph breaks very frequently occur at the same place as the paragraph breaks in the two Hebrew manuscripts of Isaiah from Qumran, as well as those in the traditional Hebrew text, reproduced in modern editions of the Hebrew Bible (the two systems are not identical, and the Peshitta represents a slightly different third tradition). Evidently the Syriac translator must have taken over the paragraph divisions from the Hebrew text he was translating. Later manuscripts of the Peshitta often introduce quite different paragraph breaks.

The earliest manuscripts have no chapter divisions. The division of books of the Peshitta Old Testament into numbered chapters (in Syriac, *shahe*) is first attested in some East Syriac manuscripts of the eighth century; subsequently this system was adopted by West Syriac scribes as well. A few manuscripts (such as the Buchanan Bible) have two concurrent systems of numbering, the first being the standard system, and the other being a cumulative system running right through the Old Testament (or group of books within the Old Testament). It should be noted that these chapter divisions only very rarely coincide with the chapter divisions familiar from modern translations of the Bible (for whose origin, see Chapter I).

Finally, before leaving the Peshitta Old Testament, we should look at the way in which the text itself has been transmitted over the centuries. On the whole one can say that Syriac scribes were generally very careful when they copied the biblical text. As a result, we find remarkably little variation between the different manuscripts (the situation is very different with the Greek Septuagint, where great variation occurs); moreover, where variants do occur, they are only rarely of much consequence. Nevertheless the Peshitta text is not entirely uniform over the centuries, and recent studies have suggested that the following is the general pattern of development in the history of the Peshitta text for each book:

1. Oldest stage. Very few witnesses to this stage survive, and often they are manuscripts which pose particular problems. It seems likely that in this oldest stage the text of the Peshitta was rather closer to the Hebrew original than is the case with the text during the later stages. If we had more manuscripts dating from the fifth century we would probably be in a better position to recover more of this archaic stage.

2. The next stage is represented by manuscripts of the sixth to eighth centuries (inclusive): since we are rather well provided with manuscripts from this time, this stage represents the earliest stage in the history of the Peshitta text which we can recover. The differences between this stage and the oldest stage (not fully recoverable) are probably the result of attempts to smooth over the original translations here and there in the interests of good Syriac idiom.

3. The third stage is provided by manuscripts of the ninth century and later, and is often referred to as the Textus Receptus, or Received Text. The differences between the Textus Receptus and the text of stage 2 are very many (there are some 50 in the whole of Isaiah), but are rarely of great significance. It remains unclear how or why this development took place—was it a gradual process, continuing the sort of changes that had already taken place between stages 1 and 2, or was it the product of a conscious revision by a particular person (and if so, by what criteria did he work)?

The following are a few typical examples of differences between stages 2 and 3, taken from Isaiah:

Isaiah 13:8: "their eyes will not have pity on their children"
   Textus Receptus has "your children."

Isaiah 52:18: "there is none who takes her by her hand"
   Textus Receptus adds "and raises her."

Isaiah 66:21: "And I will also take from them priests and Levites"
   Textus Receptus omits "And."

Most of the changes are very minor, and are introduced in order to achieve smoother reading.

The Paris manuscript of the entire Peshitta Bible (Paris syr 341, 8al) is of interest in this connection, for the text copied by the original scribe belongs to stage 2, but at some later date someone else has come along and systematically altered the text in order to make it conform to the Textus Receptus (stage 3).

In the course of the later Middle Ages the Textus Receptus itself underwent some further developments, mostly involving very minor changes (probably due to the inadvertence of scribes). It so happens that the earliest printed editions of the Syriac Bible employed late manuscripts, and so their text represents the latest stage in the history of the development of the Peshitta text.

Old Testament (2) Syro-Hexapla

Although several different early manuscripts of parts of the Syro-hexapla survive, these do not cover the entire Old Testament: the two earliest Syro-hexapla manuscripts (Add 14442 with parts of Genesis; Add. 12134 with Exodus) were both written in the seventh century, thus less than eighty or so years away from the date of Paul of Tella's original translation. Some Syro-hexapla manuscripts contain single books, while others have groups of books.

The most famous Syro-hexapla manuscript, however, is an enormous manuscript containing the second half of the Old Testament, in the Ambrosian Library, Milan (ms C 313 Inf.): it is usually dated to the late eight or early ninth century, and since the Syro-hexapla is translated from Greek, it is not surprising that the order of the biblical books is the one found in many manuscripts of the Septuagint, namely Psalms, Job, Proverbs, Ecclesiastes, Song of Songs, Wisdom of Solomon, Ben Sira, 12 Minor Prophets, Jeremiah, Baruch, Lamentations, Letter of Jeremiah, Daniel, Susanna, Bel and the Dragon, Ezekiel, and Isaiah. The manuscript is written in a beautiful Estrangelo hand, and in the margins are large numbers of notes, usually providing variant readings derived from other columns of Origen's Hexapla. In the sixteenth century the Syriac scholar Andreas Masius had the use of another huge Syro-hexapla manuscript which contained the first half of the Old Testament, but unfortunately this precious manuscript has subsequently disappeared and must be presumed lost for good.

The Ambrosian manuscript of the Syro-hexapla has a system of chapter numbering which is quite different from the one found in Peshitta manuscripts: it derives from one of the several current Greek systems, and the Greek name *kephalaion*, "chapter" (literally "heading"), is employed. Rather surprisingly a later scribe has introduced this system into the margin of one famous Peshitta manuscript, the complete Bible, 7al, also now in Milan.

We shall pass over here the two other translations of the Old Testament, made from Greek, the one possibly sponsored by Philoxenus, the other made the Jacob of Edessa in his old age. Both these survive in fragmentary form, in old manuscripts.

New Testament (1) Diatessaron

No biblical manuscript containing any part of the Syriac Diatessaron survives, and the text has to be reconstructed from the quotations from the Diatessaron incorporated into Ephrem's Commentary on the Diatessaron (which itself does not survive compete in Syriac).

New Testament (2) Old Syriac

We have already seen that the Old Syriac survives in two fifth-century manuscripts, the Curetonian and the Sinaiticus. Neither of these is preserved in a compete state.

The Curetonian manuscript comes from the Syrian Monastery in the Nitrian Desert and only a few years ago a missing leaf from the manuscript (now in London, Add. 14451) was discovered among the Syriac manuscripts still remaining in the monastery (three further leaves had found their way to Berlin much earlier). The Gospels are arranged in an unusual order, Mathew, Mark, John, Luke.

The Sinaiticus (St. Catherine's Monastery, Sinai, ms syr. 30) was discovered in 1892 by Mrs. Agnes Smith Lewis, a remarkable and very learned Scottish lady who made many discoveries of biblical and other manuscripts in the Middle East during the course of her travels with her twin sister, Mrs. Margaret Smith Gibson. The original manuscript containing the text of the Old Syriac Gospels was recycled by a certain John the Anchorite in AD 779: the original writing was sponged off, and the leaves were reused to form a new codex in which a totally different text was copied (Lives of some women saints). The manuscript as we know it today is thus a palimpsest, with the Old Syriac as the underwriting. Fortunately, a certain amount of the underwriting still shows through, and thanks to a great deal of patience, it was eventually possible publish quite a large amount of this under-writing containing the Old Syriac Gospel text. It is to be hoped that modern techniques for reading palimpsests will before long enable scholars to read rather more of this text which is of such interest for biblical studies.

New Testament (3) Peshitta

Quite a large number of manuscripts from the sixth (and a few from the fifth) century survive; normally these contain just the Gospels (and many of them survive only in a fragmentary state), but one of the earliest dated manuscripts is one containing the Pauline Epistles (AD 533/4). Perhaps the most famous of early Peshitta New Testament manuscripts is a Gospel manuscript dated AD 586, in the Laurentian Library, Florence; this contains a remarkable set of illustrations, executed by the monk Rabbula (hence the manuscript is often referred to as "the Rabbula Gospels"; this Rabbula should of course be carefully distinguished from Rabbula, bishop of Edessa).

The three Catholic Epistles (James, 1 Peter, 1 John) normally come between Acts and the Pauline Epistles, but the order of the Pauline Epistles is the same as the order familiar from the Greek and from modern translations. Sometimes at the ends of the individual Gospels and Pauline Epistles short historical notes are given, such as "Ended is the preaching of Mark, which he uttered in Latin in Rome," or "Ended is the Letter to the Romans, which was written from Corinth at the hands of Phoebe the deaconess." Though such notices are not historically reliable, they are of interest since they show what views were current in the sixth century or so.

As is the case in the Peshitta Old Testament, there is remarkably little variation in text between different manuscripts of the Peshitta New Testament. Only in a few Gospel manuscripts can traces be found of the earlier Old Syriac version. One of the few major variants, at Hebrews 2:9, has already been mentioned, at an earlier stage.

New Testament (4) Philoxenian

In the past scholars have occasionally tried to identify particular manuscripts as containing the Philoxenian version, but these attempts were misguided, and it is now realized that no manuscripts of the Philoxenian survive, with the possible exception of those which contain the sixth-century translation of the books absent from the Peshitta Canon. Our only direct access to the Philoxenian is thus by way of the quotations made from it which can be found in Philoxenus' commentaries and other works.

The sixth-century translation of the four Catholic Epistles absent from the Peshitta (2 Peter, 2–3 John, Jude) is preserved in a fairly small number of manuscripts of which the oldest is dated AD 823. Most of these manuscripts contain the rest of the New Testament in the Peshitta version as well (this, for example is the case with the Buchanan Bible). For

Revelation, however the sixth-century translation is preserved in a single manuscript, dating from the twelfth or thirteenth century. As was mentioned earlier, it is not certain whether these anonymous translations are to be identified as part of the Philoxenian New Testament or not.

New Testament (5) Harclean

The vast majority of manuscripts of the Harclean version contain only the Gospels. Several of these belong to the eighth or ninth centuries. For the rest of the New Testament, by contrast, we are not at all well off: for Revelation a small number of manuscripts are available but only two manuscripts (Oxford, New College 333, of the eleventh century, and Cambridge, Add. 1700, of 1169/70) are definitely known to have the Harclean text of both Acts and the Epistles as well. Recently, an earlier manuscript (of the eighth or ninth century, in the library of St Mark's Monastery, Jerusalem) has been identified as containing the Epistles in the Harclean version.

2. LECTIONARIES

The Bible was read in the context of liturgical worship from the very beginnings of the existence of the Church (at first of course, it was just the Old Testament, before the written New Testament had come into being). In the early centuries of the Church's life biblical manuscripts containing the relevant parts of Scripture were used. In the sixth century some Syriac biblical manuscripts provided help in locating lections by inserting lectionary headings (sometimes in red) at the beginning of passages to be read on particular feasts. Sometimes lists of reading throughout the liturgical year were compiled, but these did not include the text of the lections; a sixth-century index of lections of this sort survives in the British Library (Add. 14528). The practice of incorporating lectionary headings at appropriate places in ordinary biblical manuscripts continued in the seventh and eighth centuries, and sometimes later as well, even after the adoption of the bright idea of having separate books, containing just the lections, and arranged in their liturgical order.

It is unknown when this idea of having a special lectionary manuscript for lections was first introduced; the earliest Greek lectionary manuscripts (all very fragmentary) seem to belong to the fifth century, but the idea does not appear to have become popular until some centuries later. Certainly in the Syriac Churches it is the case that there are no Syriac lectionary manuscripts dating from earlier than the ninth century. It is of course possible that earlier lectionary manuscripts did once exist, and that they have disappeared simply because they had more wear and tear than ordinary biblical manuscripts; this suggestion, however, should probably be rejected, for two reasons: (1) since biblical manuscripts of the sixth and seventh century were provided with lectionary headings, they too would have been subject to the same wear and tear; (2) we suddenly have quite a lot of lectionary manuscripts dating from the ninth century, and belonging to all three Churches using Syriac as a liturgical language—the Syrian Orthodox, the Church of the East, and the Byzantine Orthodox (Melkite) Church in Syria and Palestine. It thus seems likely that the practice of collecting together the lections into special manuscripts was introduced into all the Syriac Churches at some time around AD 800.

Since different parts of the Bible were read at different points in the liturgical services, it became the usual practice to have separate lectionaries for Old Testament lections, for Gospel lections, and for lections from the Acts and the Epistles. The text employed in lectionaries was normally the Peshitta, but in the Syrian Orthodox Church use was also sometimes made of the Syro-hexapla and of the Harclean. In particular, there are many Harclean Gospel lectionaries which survive. In some Gospel lectionary manuscripts a harmony has been created for the Passion narrative, based on the text of the Harclean; two different sequences are attested, and one of these is associated (in a colophon) with the names of a certain Rabban Mar Daniel and his disciple Isaac.

There appears to have been considerable variation in the allocation and arrangement of lections, not only between the different Syriac Churches, but also within each of the Churches. In the Church of the East two particular systems in due course came to dominate the scene: firstly the "Cathedral" lectionary system of the patriarchal church formerly in Seleucia-Ctesiphon, and secondly the monastic lectionary cycle developed at the Upper Monastery in Mosul; eventually the monastic system almost completely displaced its 'cathedral' counterpart.

3. PRINTED EDITIONS

The first printed edition of the Syriac New Testament was published by Johann Widmanstetter in 1555 at Vienna. In the work of preparing the edition Widmanstetter had been assisted by the Syrian Orthodox priest, Moses of Mardin, who spent some time in Europe acting as a teacher of Syriac to various scholars. The text of this edition was often reprinted, sometimes in Hebrew characters.

For the Peshitta Old Testament the earliest printed editions were of the Psalter; the first was prepared by Maronites in 1610, at Quzhaya (Lebanon) to be followed shortly afterwards by two other editions both of which were published in 1625, one in Leiden prepared by Thomas Erpenius, and the other in Paris prepared by the Maronite scholar Gabriel Sionita.

The next two Syriac biblical texts to be published were not from the Peshitta, but from one of the later versions. In 1627 Louis de Dieu published the Harclean Apocalypse (Leiden), and in 1630 Edward Pococke published the four minor Catholic Epistles which are missing from the Peshitta (Oxford); the version he published was the anonymous sixth-century one, rather than the Harclean (in later literature on the Syriac versions they are often referred to as the "Pococke Epistles"). None of these texts of course featured in Widmanstetter's edition of the Peshitta New Testament, and their absence had surprised and shocked European scholars.

The complete Old Testament Peshitta was first published in volumes 6–9 of the great "Paris Polyglot" (1645), edited by G. M. Le Jay; the edition of the Syriac text was the work of Gabriel Sionita. The Paris Polyglot also included the Syriac New Testament, supplementing the Peshitta text with the "Pococke Epistles" and the Harclean Apocalypse.

The Syriac text of the Paris Polyglot served as the basis for the next edition of the Peshitta Bible, in Brian Walton's London Polyglot (1655–7).

In both the Polyglot Bibles the Syriac text is provided with a Latin translation. Their text is not a very good one since very late manuscripts (all West Syrian) were employed as the basis.

The next important edition of the Syriac Bible was that prepared by Samuel Lee, published in London in 1823. Although the text was mostly derived from Walton's Polyglot, some use was made of the Buchanan Bible in preparing this influential edition. The Old Testament text is unvocalized but the New Testament is vocalized. The contents of the Old Testament were dictated by the contents of the King James Version of the Bible (the "Apocrypha" are absent), though the order of the books in part follows patterns found in Peshitta manuscripts: thus, for example, Job comes between Deuteronomy and Joshua. In the New Testament, however, the standard order of edition of the Greek text (and of modern translations) was followed, that is, with the Pauline Epistles following immediately after Acts. For the books absent from the Peshitta, the "Pococke Epistles" and the Harclean Apocalypse are employed. An interesting feature of this edition of the New Testament is the presence of numerous lectionary headings, which have been taken over from one of the manuscripts which Lee used.

Lee's edition has been re-issued by the United Bible Societies (1979), in an expanded form, and with a brief preface by the Syrian Orthodox Patriarch Ignatius Ya'qub III. The added material is the text of the Deutero-canonical books, under the title "Books of the Apocrypha"; these are reproduced from handwriting (Serto) and include the following: Wisdom of Solomon, Ben Sira, 2 Letters of Baruch, Letter of Jeremiah, 1–2 Maccabees, Tobit, Judith, supplements to Esther, Susanna.

The first printed edition of the Peshitta based at least in part on East Syrian manuscripts was published in Urmia (northwestern Iran) in 1852 by the American Presbyterian Mission. The edition has a Modern Syriac translation (from Hebrew, rather than from the Peshitta) in parallel columns. The Urmia edition served as the basis for another edition using the East Syrian script, published by the Trinitarian Bible Society in New York (1913) and often reprinted. Both these editions follow the order of books familiar from most English translations.

Another edition of the Peshitta using East Syrian manuscripts (and including the New Testament) was published by the Dominican Fathers at Mosul in 1887–92 (in three volumes): this had been prepared by Clement Joseph David, Syrian Catholic Archbishop of Damascus, and George Abdisho Khayyat, Chaldaean Archbishop of Amid (Diyarbekir). The order of the Old Testament books is the same as that of the Urmia edition, but inserted among them are the so-called Deutero-canonical books (absent from Protestant Bibles), such as Wisdom of Solomon and Ben Sira (between the Song of Songs and Isaiah). The New Testament follows the standard Greek order; for the books not in the Peshitta use is made of the "Pococke Epistles" and the Harclean Revelation.

The Beirut edition of the Peshitta (1952) is largely based on the Mosul edition.

All the editions mentioned so far are based on late and often not very good manuscripts. For most purposes this may not matter very much, but for more scholarly purposes it is obviously important to have a more reliable text of the Peshitta available, based on the oldest manuscripts. This is essential, for example, if one wishes to study the Peshitta Old Testament as a translation of the Hebrew.

In the last century or so various attempts have been made by scholars to produce better editions of the Syriac Bible. The following are some of the more important:

(a) Old Testament (Peshitta)

- Beginning in 1876 A. M. Ceriani started to publish a photo-lithographic reproduction of the Old Testament text of the famous Ambrosian manuscript of the Peshitta (7a1); this work, completed in 1883, made available for the first time the text of the oldest surviving manuscript of the complete Peshitta Old Testament.

- Various scholars have prepared editions of individual books of the Peshitta Old Testament based on the oldest manuscripts available. These include: the Pentateuch (W. E. Barnes, 1914; a revision of the text in Lee's edition using old manuscripts) Psalms (W. E. Barnes, 1904); Isaiah (G. Diettrich, 1905; no text is given, but there is a full list of variant readings to be found in 22 manuscripts is given); Lamentations (B. Albrektson, 1963); Chronicles (W. E. Barnes, 1897; list of variant readings in several early manuscripts, without the text); Apocrypha (P. de Lagarde, 1861; based on early manuscripts in the British Library); Wisdom of Solomon (J. A. Emerton, 1959); Ben Sira (N. Calduch-Benages and others, 2003).

- In the 1950s the International Organisation for the Study of the Old Testament began to make plans for a critical edition of the Peshitta Old Testament, and in 1959 Professor P. A. H. de Boer, of the University of Leiden in Holland, was appointed general editor. In 1961 the new Peshitta Institute at Leiden published a preliminary List of Old Testament Peshitta Manuscripts, prepared largely by W. Baars and M. D. Koster. (Every now and then supplements to this invaluable basic list have been published in the periodical *Vetus Testamentum*). Five years later, in 1966, a sample edition containing the Song of Songs, Tobit, and the Apocalypse of Baruch was published. Over the following years the following volumes have appeared:

I   1   Genesis and Exodus (ed. T. Jansma, M. D. Koster, 1977).

II   2   Judges and Samuel (ed. P. B. Dirksen, P. A. H. de Boer, 1978).

II   3   Psalms (ed. D. M. Walter and others, 1980).

II   4   Kings (ed. H. Gottlieb and E. Hammershaimb, 1976).

II   5   Proverbs, Wisdom of Solomon, Ecclesiastes, Song of Songs (ed. A. A. di Lella, J. A. Emerton, D. J. Lane).

III   1   Isaiah (ed. S. P. Brock, 1987).

III 1a Job (ed. L. G. Rignell, 1982).

III 3 Ezekiel (ed. M. J. Mulder, 1985).

III 4 Twelve Prophets, Daniel, Bel and the Dragon (ed. A. Gelston, T. Sprey, 1980).

IV 2 Chronicles (ed. R. P. Gordon, 1998).

IV 3 Apocalypse of Baruch and 4 Esdras (ed. R. J. Bidawid, 1973).

IV 6 Canticles or Odes, Prayer of Manasseh, Apocryphal Psalms, Psalms of Solomon, Tobit, 1 (3) Esdras (ed. H. Schneider, W. Baars, J. C. H. Lebram, 1972).

It is hoped to complete the edition some time in the near future. Estrangelo script is used throughout. The text printed is basically that of the Ambrosian manuscript, 7a1, though its manifest errors are corrected. Below the text there is an apparatus which gives all the variants to be found in manuscripts before 1300 (obvious errors and orthographical differences are excluded there, but receive mention in the introductions to each volume, where the manuscripts used are described). Editions earlier than 1977 give variants in later manuscripts as well, and the text in these volumes adheres more rigidly to 7a1 than is the case in later volumes. The importance of the Leiden edition lies in the fact that it provides for the first time information about the earliest forms of the Peshitta text, before the development of the medieval Textus Receptus (which is the basis of all the older editions of the Peshitta Bible).

(b) New Testament (Peshitta)

• For the Peshitta Gospels an edition (with facing Latin translation) based on a considerable number of the earliest surviving manuscripts was prepared by P. E. Pusey and published (after Pusey's death) by G. H. Gwilliam in 1901. The intention had been to cover the rest of the New Testament, but this never came to fruition; the provisional text for this edition, however, was published, without any variant readings, by the British and Foreign Bible Society in 1920. This edition of the Peshitta New Testament, printed in vocalized Serto script, is the most reliable one available, and it has been reprinted many times. The Syriac order of books is followed, with James, I Peter, and I John coming after Acts. Use was made of the anonymous sixth-century translation for the minor Catholic Epistles (the "Pococke Epistles") and Revelation, since these are absent from the Peshitta; the text of these was based on the excellent editions by J. Gwynn (minor Catholic Epistles, 1909; Revelation, 1897). These are all printed together at the end. For odd verses absent from the Peshitta (notably John 7:53–8:11) a later translation has been inserted between square brackets. Besides the Western chapter and verse numbers, the native Syriac section numbers ("*shahe*") are given in the margin (these very rarely correspond with the Western chapter divisions).

- In 1983 The Way International (New Knoxville, Ohio, USA) published a volume entitled "The Aramaic New Testament, Estrangelo script, based on the Peshitta and Harklean Versions." The Peshitta text is 'taken from three early manuscripts in the British Library, but for the books absent from the Peshitta, the text of Gwynn's editions of the anonymous sixth-century versions is used (the title page and Introduction mistakenly call them the Harclean). The order of books follows that of editions of the Greek text and of modern translations. Though in many ways this is a practical edition with a good text and clearly printed, the absence of any punctuation marks (beyond verse divisions) makes for difficult reading, especially in the Epistles.

- The Institut für Neutestamentliche Text Forschung at Münster (West Germany) is in the process of editing the Syriac New Testament in both the Peshitta and the Harclean versions. This important scholarly enterprise, entitled *Das Neue Testament in syrischer Überlieferung*, has so far published the Catholic Epistles (James, 1 Peter, 1 John), and the Pauline Epistles (Berlin, 1986-2002). For the Peshitta a selected group of nine early manuscripts has been used, while for the Harclean all available manuscripts are employed. A notable feature of this edition is the extensive use made of quotations from the New Testament in Syriac writers. The text of the Peshitta, Harclean, and the various quotations is set out line by line so that one can immediately see the difference between them. Each volume has a long introduction dealing with the transmission of the text and the relationships between the Syriac texts and their underlying Greek originals.

A major event in the history of editions of the Syriac Bible was the publication, in 1996, of George Kiraz's four-volume *Comparative*

Edition of the Syriac Gospels, which provides an aligned text of the two Old Syriac manuscripts, the Peshitta, and the Harclean .

For anyone interested in studying the ways in which Syriac biblical translations developed over the course of some five centuries, these two comparative editions, of the Gospels and of the Epistles, provide a wonderfully convenient resource, and a careful perusal of them will prove to be most instructive.

(c) Main Syriac Versions Other Than The Peshitta

For the Syro-hexapla the most important editions are:

- the photo-lithographic edition of the Milan manuscript (C. 313 Inf.) containing the second half of the Syro-hexapla, published by A. M. Ceriani (1874).

- the collection of all Syro-hexapla texts available for the first half of the Old Testament by P. de Lagarde and A. Rahlfs (*Bibliothecae Syriacae*, 1892).

- a collection of *New Syro-Hexaplaric Texts*, edited by W. Baars (1968, with a valuable introduction on the history of earlier editions).

- a photographic edition, by A. Vööbus, of a Syro-hexapla manuscript of the Pentateuch dated 1204 (1975).

For the anonymous sixth-century version of the minor Catholic Epistles and Revelation, mention has already been made of the editions by Gwynn (1897 for Revelation, 1905 for the minor Catholic Epistles).

The only edition of the Harclean New Testament was published long ago by J. White (Gospels, 1778; Acts and Epistles, 1799, 1803). The work was given the misleading title *Versio Syriaca Philoxeniana*; today, however, it is known for certain that the text of White's edition is the Harclean, and not the Philoxenian. The end of White's manuscript is lost, and so his edition ends at Hebrews 11:27. The rest of Hebrews was published from another manuscript by R. Bensly (1889). The Harclean text of Revelation, first published by L. De Dieu in 1627, appears in most subsequent editions of the Syriac New Testament published in the eighteenth and nineteenth centuries. A photographic edition of a further manuscript of the Harclean text of Revelation has recently been published by A. Vööbus (1978). For the Gospels there is now a much better text of the Harclean available in G. Kiraz's *Comparative Edition of the Syriac Gospels*, for which A. Juckel provided the text based on one of the oldest Harclean Gospel manuscripts; likewise for the Epistles there is also a much more reliable text in B. Aland and A. Juckel's *Das Neue Testament in syrischer Überlieferung* I and II.1-3. There is also a separate edition of the Harclean text of St. John (G. H. Bernstein, 1853).

(d) Tools

There are no complete concordances to the Syriac Bible available yet. For the Peshitta Old Testament there are a number of concordances to individual groups of books available (mostly prepared by W. Strothmann and assistants); these are based on some of the older printed editions.

A concordance to the Peshitta New Testament was prepared by A. Bonus, but this has never been published. The so-called *Concordance to the Peshitta Version of the Aramaic New Testament* (1985) is in fact not a concordance, but a word list. Fortunately the Peshitta New Testament has now recently been excellently served by George Kiraz's *A Computer-Generated Concordance to the Syriac New Testament* (6 vols, Leiden, 1993), and the Old Syriac Gospels by J. Lund's *The Old Syriac Gospel of the Distinct Evangelists. A Key-Word-in-Context Concordance* (3 vols, Piscataway NJ, 2004). A handy Syriac-English dictionary to the Syriac New Testament was published by W. Jennings (1926). For anyone interested in the relationship of the Peshitta Gospels to the Greek, T. Falla's *A Key to the Peshitta Gospels* will be very useful; of this only volumes I and II have appeared so far (Leiden, 1996, 2000), covering from *alaph* to *yodh*). Another useful recent dictionary to the entire Peshitta New Testament has been provided by M. Pazzini, *Lessico concordanziale del Nuovo Testamento Siriaco* (Jerusalem, 2004).

4. TRANSLATIONS

The Peshitta has been translated into a number of different languages over the course of its history; most of these are old ones, such as translations into Persian and Sogdian (only fragments of these survive). Many translations of different parts of the Peshitta into Arabic were made in the Middle Ages, and one sometimes finds (especially in lectionary manuscripts) the Syriac and Arabic in parallel columns (the Arabic often written in Syriac script, known as Karshuni).

In the Polyglot editions of the Bible the Peshitta text was provided with a Latin translation.

The only complete English translation of the Peshitta is by G. Lamsa. This is unfortunately not always very accurate, and his claims that the Peshitta Gospels represent the Aramaic original underlying the Greek Gospels are entirely without foundation; such views, which are not infrequently found in more popular literature, are rejected by all serious scholars.

There is an older English translation of the Peshitta New Testament by James Murdock (1893).

A good modern translation of the Peshitta, or at least of passages used in the lectionary, is very much needed. For the Peshitta Old Testament there are plans for a group of scholars to produce and English translation based on the oldest manuscripts.

There seem to be at least three translations of the Peshitta New Testament into Malayalam.

CHAPTER IV

BIBLICAL INTERPRETATION IN THE SYRIAC TRADITION

The Bible can be interpreted on many different levels. For our present purpose it will be sufficient to follow the practice of several Syriac writers and to distinguish between two different modes of interpretation. St. Ephrem already makes the distinction between "factual" and "spiritual" interpretation (today we might prefer to call the first of these "historical"). The factual or historical interpretation is primarily concerned with illuminating the circumstances surrounding episodes in the Bible: who were the people involved, when and where did they live, and so on. The spiritual interpretation, on the other hand, is concerned with the eternal truths underlying the text; it seeks to penetrate beyond the surface meaning to the various inner meanings.

Where historical interpretation is concerned we are dealing with facts, and we can speak of a historical interpretation as being "correct" or "incorrect," or as "right" or "wrong" (though often we do not have sufficient evidence to decide conclusively between the two). This is quite different from the situation with spiritual interpretation: here it is not a case of one interpretation being right and another wrong, for there is never one "correct" interpretation to the exclusion of all others. Often several spiritual interpretations may be simultaneously valid. For a spiritual interpretation to be valid, it must be meaningful in a particular context; and to be meaningful, it must provide insight on the world of objective spiritual truth or reality. These two criteria are important: the first helps us to realize that the same spiritual interpretation may be valid (that is, meaningful) to one person, but not to another; or it may be meaningful to the same person at one time, but not at another. The second criterion is important because spiritual interpretation which provides insight on objective spiritual truth is much more likely to be found within orthodox Christian tradition than in some other form of Christianity which is given to an individualistic and highly subjective interpretation of Scripture.

Historical and spiritual interpretation of Scripture thus operate in very different ways, each with its own mode of operation. Historical interpretation provides us with the outer meaning, spiritual interpretation directs us towards the inner meaning of the biblical text. The two approaches should complement one another, but all too often their proper roles have been misunderstood, and the criteria belonging to the one have been misguidedly applied to the other. This has given rise to all sorts of misconceptions, such as the idea that biblical scholarship is dangerous or harmful to faith. Much more dangerous, and spiritually harmful, is the fundamentalist approach to the Bible which confuses spiritual truth with historical truth, thus creating a totally unnecessary conflict between religion and science.

With these rather lengthy preliminaries we can now turn to the Syrian interpretation of Scripture. The Syriac Fathers are interested both in "factual," or "historical," and in "spiritual" interpretation, though not surprisingly they pay greater attention to the latter. Since modern historical understanding of the Bible and its background is vastly superior to that of the Syriac Fathers (thanks to the advances in biblical scholarship over the last century), what the Syriac Fathers have to say on the level of historical interpretation is very rarely of more than antiquarian interest. What they have to say in the area of spiritual interpretation, however, has by no means been superseded, and much of what they say can be just as meaningful today as it was to their own times. Accordingly, we shall primarily be looking at examples of their spiritual interpretation.

A number of passages in the writings of St. Ephrem (d. 373) provide us with excellent guidance on how Scripture should be read. On the one hand he sees the Scriptures themselves as possessing an unfathomable depth of "hidden power" (that is, spiritual meaning; Western writers would probably prefer to speak of divine inspiration). On the other hand, in order for the Christian to be able to draw on these hidden depths of spiritual meaning, he or she must read the Bible with "the eye of faith," that is, with an openness to the guidance of the Holy Spirit, for this same Spirit will then lead the reader to discover "the power which lies hidden" within the words of the biblical text. Thus, for the Bible to "come to life" and to become spiritually meaningful there is need for openness to, and co-operation with, the Spirit on the part of the reader (or hearer) of the Bible, for only then will the reader become aware of the spiritual truths hidden within the Scripture. Thus St. Ephrem says in one of his hymns, "The Scriptures are laid out like a mirror, and he whose eye is lucid sees within them the mirror of Truth" (Hymns on Faith 67:8).

St. Ephrem says emphatically on a number of occasions that it is wrong to read the Bible in a literal way, for this will lead to all sorts of misconceptions. Thus, for example, in one of his Hymns on Paradise (11:6) he says,

If someone concentrates his attention solely
    on the metaphors which are used of God's majesty,
he then abuses and misrepresents that majesty
    and thus errs
by means of those same metaphors
    with which God has clothed himself for man's own benefit;
such a person is ungrateful to God's grace
    which has bent down its stature
to the level of human childishness:
    Even though God has nothing in common with humanity
nevertheless he clothed himself in the likeness of humanity
    in order to bring humanity to the likeness of himself.

Ephrem often speaks of God as "clothing himself in names (or metaphors)" in the Old Testament, as a prelude to his "clothing himself in the human body" at the Incarnation. But we should not abuse God's condescension in making himself known to humanity in this way by taking these metaphors literally:

Let us give thanks to God who clothed himself in the names of the
        body's various parts:
Scripture refers to his 'ears', to teach us that he listens to us;
it speaks of his 'eyes', to show that he see us.
It was just the names of such things that he put on.
Although in his true Being there is no wrath or regret,
    yet he put on these names too, because of our weakness.

We should realize that, if he had not put on the names of such things,
    it would not have been possible for him to speak with us humans:
he drew close to us by means of what belongs to us;
he clothed himself in our language, so that he might clothe us in his
        mode of life,
He asked for our form (Philippians 2:7) and put this on;
then, as a father with his children, he spoke with our childish state.

It is our metaphors that he put on—though he did not literally do so!
He then took them off—without actually doing so: when wearing them,
        he was at the same time stripped of them;
he puts one on when it is beneficial, then strips it off to exchange it for
        another.

The fact that he strips off and puts on all sorts of metaphors
tells us that the metaphor does not apply to this true Being;
because that Being is hidden, he has depicted it by means of what is
        visible.

(Hymns on Faith 31:1-3)

A passage of Scripture is capable of only one correct historical interpretation at a time; such a restriction, however, does not apply to spiritual interpretation: in that case, the more lucid and luminous the inner eye of faith is, the more spiritual interpretations it will be capable of discovering. As Ephrem points out, it would be very boring if a passage of Scripture had only one spiritual meaning:

> If there only existed a single sense for the words of Scripture, then the first commentator who came along would discover it, and other hearers would experience neither the labor of searching, nor the joy of discovery. Rather, each word of our Lord has its own form, and each form has its own members, and each member has its own character. And each individual person understands according to his capacity, and he interprets the passages as is granted to him.

(Commentary on the Diatessaron 7:22).

Earlier in the Commentary on the Diatessaron St. Ephrem has the following excellent advice (in the first paragraph he addresses Christ):

> Who is capable of comprehending the extent of what is to be discovered in a single utterance of yours? For we leave behind in it far more than we take away from it, like thirsty people drinking from a fountain.

> The facets of God's word are far more numerous than the faces of those who learn from it. God depicted his word with many beauties, so that each of those who learn from it can examine that aspect of it which he likes. And God has hidden within his word all sorts of treasures, so that each of us can be enriched by it, from whatever aspect he meditates on. For God's word is the Tree of Life which extends to you blessed fruits from every direction; it is like the Rock which was struck in the Wilderness, which became a spiritual drink for everyone on all sides: "They ate the food of the Spirit and they drank the draft of the Spirit."

> Anyone who encounters Scripture should not suppose that the single one of its riches that he has found is the only one to exist; rather, he should realize that he himself is only capable of discovering that one out of the many riches which exist in it.

Nor, because Scripture has enriched him, should the reader impoverish it. Rather, if the reader is incapable of finding more, let him acknowledge Scripture's magnitude. Rejoice because you have found satisfaction, and do not be grieved that there has been something left over by you. A thirsty person rejoices because he has drunk: he is not grieved because he proved incapable of drinking the fountain dry. Let the fountain vanquish your thirst: your thirst should not try to vanquish the fountain! If your thirst comes to an end while the fountain has not been diminished, then you can drink again whenever you are thirsty; whereas, if the fountain had been drained dry once you had had your fill, your victory over it would have proved to be for your own harm. Give thanks for what you have taken away, and do not complain about the superfluity that is left over. What you have taken off with you is your portion; what has been left behind can still become your inheritance.

(Commentary on the Diatessaron 1:18-19)

The type of spiritual interpretation which is employed most frequently by the Syriac Fathers can best be described as typological or symbolic interpretation. This kind of interpretation can already be found in the New Testament, where, for example, St. Paul speaks of Christ as "the latter Adam" (1 Cor 15:45). Typology is in fact a means of indicating relationships: relationships between the Old Testament and the New, between the New Testament and the Church, between the material world and the heavenly world, between historical events and persons in Scripture and their spiritual meaning. Types and symbols serve as pointers: from the standpoint of subjective human perspective, a type or symbol can be seen as a means of revealing some aspect of objective divine reality (Truth, in Ephrem's terminology); alternately, from the standpoint of objective divine perspective, a type or symbol is a place in which some aspect of divine reality lies hidden. Although the Greek word for type, "*typos*," does sometimes occur in Syriac, the normal term used for type or symbol is "*raza*," which properly means "mystery," but which is usually best translated in this context as "symbol," though it should be stressed that "symbol" has a much stronger meaning than the one current in modern English, where a symbol is usually sharply distinguished from the thing it symbolizes. For the Syriac Fathers the link between symbol and the reality symbolized is intimate, for in the symbol there resides the "hidden power" of the reality.

The verse John 19:34 is a passage which excellently illustrates the mechanics, as it were, of typological exegesis. The Peshitta has here: "But one of the soldiers struck him on his side with a spear, and immediately there came forth blood and water." With the help of typology the piercing of Christ's side on the Cross is linked backwards to the Genesis narrative of the fall of Adam and his expulsion from Paradise, and forwards to the sacramental life of the Church; in other words, the typological interpretation of this verse points to the true significance of the crucifixion and its importance as the turning point in the whole of salvation history. How does it achieve this?

First, the links with the Genesis narrative are provided by the following contrasted elements:

- the side of Christ the Second Adam, and the rib, or side, of the First Adam (Gen 2:21–2), whence Eve was extracted;

- the spear which pierced Christ, and the fiery sword which kept the Adam out of Paradise (Gen 3:24).

The piercing of Christ's side with the spear can thus be seen as removing the fiery sword which has hitherto kept Adam (humanity) out of Paradise; in other words, the crucifixion opens up the possibility for humanity to return to the original state of Paradise.

Secondly, links forward to the Church are provided by:

- the blood, a symbol of the Eucharist;

- the water, a symbol of Baptism.

Moving on from here a further step, the Syriac Fathers speak of the Church (as the place where the Sacraments of Baptism and the Eucharist are found) coming forth, or being born, from the side of Christ. This in turn provides a contrast to Eve, who was "born" from the side of the First Adam. The image of birthgiving then allows the introduction of another set of relationships: the birth of Eve from Adam and the birth of the Church from Christ were both virgin births (as too was the birth of Adam from the Earth), and this of course introduces the virgin birth of Christ from Mary, herself the Second Eve.

We are thus provided with an extremely intricate web of typological relationships which help to show how every point in salvation history is interlinked, and how we today are ourselves participants in this history through the sacraments of Baptism and the Eucharist. The typological parallelism implied in this network of interrelationships between Mary and the Church also provides fruitful and suggestive material for theological meditation.

Such, in prosaic terms, is the bare skeletal framework upon which the typological interpretation of John 19:34 functions. For the skeleton to come to life, one needs to read some of the passages where the Syriac Fathers have breathed life into these bare bones.

It is significant that much of the best spiritual interpretation of the Bible among the Syriac Fathers is to be found in poetry rather than in prose. Thus the poems of Ephrem, Narsai, and Jacob of Serugh will appear today as far more creative in their spiritual interpretation of Scripture than the many later prose commentaries which survive.

CHAPTER V

BIBLICAL COMMENTARIES

Commentaries on the Bible can take many forms. The earlier Syriac commentaries are generally on one particular book at a time, whereas from the eighth and ninth century onwards it became the fashion to provide commentaries on the whole Bible.

The earliest surviving Syriac commentaries are those by Ephrem (ca. 306–373), and it is quite likely that they date from the last ten years of his life, spent at Edessa. The following are generally agreed to be by Ephrem himself (though in some cases it is possible that his disciples published them in their present form):

- Commentary on Genesis and most of Exodus; this survives in Syriac in a unique manuscript. The Commentary follows the order of the biblical text, but only selected passages are commented on. The early chapters of Genesis receive much more attention than the later ones, and Ephrem shows great interest in the question of human free will. There is very little typological interpretation; this contrasts with the typological interpretation given to many passages from Genesis and Exodus in his hymns. Throughout the commentary many intriguing links with Jewish exegetical traditions are to be found.

- Commentary on the Diatessaron. This survives complete in an early translation into Armenian; in recent times about two-thirds of the Syriac original have been recovered and published (1963; 1990, after some further leaves of the same manuscript had come to light). The Commentary follows the sequence of the Diatessaron (and since the Syriac Diatessaron is lost, the Commentary is an extremely important witness to both its text and structure); as in the Genesis and Exodus Commentary, Ephrem is selective in the passages upon which he chooses to comment, but the commentary itself is much more theological in character; furthermore many passages are meditative in character.

- Commentary on Acts. This comparatively short work survives only in an Armenian translation.

73

- Commentary on the Pauline Epistles. This too survives only in an Armenian translation. A curious feature of this Commentary is Ephrem's inclusion of a non-canonical letter attributed to Paul, known as 3 Corinthians. This letter was evidently quite widely read in the early Syriac Church, but later fell out of favor (it is clearly not genuine).

Thanks to Ephrem's enormous reputation, many works not by him came to be attributed to him. This applies to almost all the commentaries on the Old Testament attributed to him in the eighteenth-century edition of his works. There are also Armenian translations of Old Testament commentaries under his name, but these turn out not to represent genuine Ephrem.

Following chronological order, probably the next Syriac commentaries to survive are certain works by John of Apamea, or John the Solitary. Much uncertainty surrounds this figure and the works under his name, which include a commentary on Ecclesiastes and one on the Beatitudes. Of these only the former has been published (by W. Strothmann), but without an accompanying translation. These are not commentaries in the modern sense; instead, John uses select passages in the biblical text as spring-boards for teaching on the spiritual life.

From the middle of the fifth century onwards Syriac commentators come under the influence of some of the main Greek commentators of the late fourth and early fifth century. These Greek writers fall into two main schools of exegesis, generally known as the Antiochene and the Alexandrian. As far as later Syriac exegetical tradition was concerned, the most important representative of the Antiochene school of exegesis was Theodore of Mopsuestia (d. 428), while for the Alexandrian school it was Cyril of Alexandria (d. 444).

The Antiochene school was particularly interested in historical interpretation, and from the point of view of modern biblical scholarship this school was the more critical in its approach, even anticipating in some respects the findings of modern critics. Representatives of this approach often adapted to the Bible techniques which had been developed by scholars of pagan Greek literary texts. Many of Theodore's works were translated into Syriac in the course of the fifth century, probably at the famous Persian School in Edessa; it was through this school, and its successor (from 489) at Nisibis, that the Antiochene exegetical tradition came to exert a pervasive influence on many Syriac writers. In the Church of the East, where Theodore was regarded as the Exegete par excellence, and where Theodore's christology was considered normative, it is no surprise to find his exegesis as dominant too. But it is also the case that Theodore and the Antiochene exegetical tradition exerted a considerable influence on writers of the Syrian Orthodox tradition like Jacob of Serugh and even Philoxenus; this happened for the simple reason that these men had once themselves been students at the Persian School, and though they reacted against its theological teaching, they nevertheless remained influenced by its tradition of biblical interpretation.

Since Theodore of Mopsuestia later came under a cloud of disapproval in the Greek Church, most of his writings have been lost in Greek. Many of his works which have managed to survive are known only from their translation into Syriac; amongst these is a long and important *Commentary on St. John's Gospel.* Quite extensive portions of his *Commentary on the Psalms* are also available in Syriac.

In passing it should be noted that a great many of John Chrysostom's exegetical homilies on different books of the Bible were translated into Syriac at an early date; to judge by the number of manuscripts which survive, these were widely read. Other works translated into Syriac were Athanasius' *Exposition of the Psalms* (in a longer and a shorter form) and Gregory of Nyssa's famous *Commentary on the Song of Songs.*

The Alexandrian exegetical tradition was distinguished from the Antiochene by its willingness to employ allegory as a method of biblical interpretation (Theodore in particular was strongly opposed to the use of allegory). It would be a mistake, however, to think that all Alexandrine interpretation is allegorical: much of it would best be described as typological, and in this respect it has much in common with its Antiochene counterpart. Alexandrine exegesis has left much less of an impression on subsequent Syriac tradition, even though Syrian Orthodox writers had available in Syriac translation several of Cyril of Alexandria's Commentaries (his *Commentary on Luke*, in the form of a series of homilies, survives only in Syriac translation).

The two great Syriac poets, Narsai (d. ca. 500) and Jacob of Serugh (d. 521) both stand in the Antiochene exegetical tradition, even though Jacob rejected Antiochene christology. Many of their verse homilies (*memre*) are in effect commentaries on particular biblical passages; both poets, for example, have a series of homilies on Creation.

Philoxenus of Mabbug (d. 523) has left commentaries on the Prologue of St. John, and on Matthew and Luke (these two survive only in fragmentary form). The commentary on the Prologue of John is in the form of an extended theological exposition.

The Church of the East produced a number of commentaries in the sixth century, but little is known of their work today. One of the more influential of these commentators was Ahob of Qatar (in the Gulf) whose work is known only from quotations in much later writers. Among the recent finds of Syriac (and other) manuscripts at St. Catherine's monastery on Mount Sinai it has been reported that there is an otherwise unknown commentary on the Bible by the great East Syrian theologian Babai (d. 628).

The chief luminary in the field of Syriac biblical exegesis in the seventh century was undoubtedly the Syrian Orthodox scholar Jacob of Edessa (d. 708). Jacob, like many West Syrian authors of his time, knew Greek well; he also knew a little Hebrew, which was exceptional for a Christian scholar of that time. He displays his knowledge of Hebrew in a long and learned note on the Tetragrammaton, the Hebrew divine name written YHWH but read as Adonay ("my Lord," for which the Septuagint has *Kyrios* and the Peshitta *Marya*, both meaning "Lord"). This particular note is attached to his revised translation of the Homilies of Severus of Antioch, but he has also left a whole series of scholia and letters on particular biblical topics in which he displays considerable critical acumen. His most important work of exegesis, however, is his *Commentary on the Six Days of Creation (Hexaemeron)*. It had become a tradition by his time for commentaries on the opening of Genesis to be the vehicle for a great deal of scientific knowledge, ranging from zoology to geography. Jacob's commentary certainly lives up to this tradition, and it is a storehouse of learning on all sorts of topics. Jacob had left the work unfinished at his death, and so it was left to his equally learned disciple George, bishop of the Arab tribes (d. 724), to complete it.

The names of several East Syrian commentators (such as Hnana of Adiabene and Gabriel of Qatar) are known from quotations in later writers, but it is not until the late eighth and the ninth century that we have surviving commentaries. From that period we have a number of important works:

- *The Book of Scholia*, by Theodore bar Koni (late eighth century); this is in the form of sets of questions and answers on select topics on every book of the Peshitta Bible. (The idea of a biblical commentary in the form of a series of Questions and Answers was taken over from Greek writers such as Theodoret). *The Book of Scholia* comes down to us in two different recensions, both of which have been published in the Louvain Corpus of Oriental Christian Writers (CSCO).

- A Commentary on the whole Bible again in the form of Questions and Answers, by Isho'barnun, Catholicus of the Church of the East from 823–828. Only the section on the Pentateuch has been published so far (by E. G. Clarke, 1962).

- An anonymous commentary on Genesis and Exodus (to 9:32); this has recently been published by L. van Rompay (1986) in the CSCO.

- An anonymous commentary on the Old and the New Testament; only the section on Genesis 1–17 has been published so far (A. Levene, 1951).

- Commentary on the Old and New Testaments by Isho'dad of Merv (flourished ca. 850). The Commentaries on the Old Testament have been published by C. van den Eynde in the CSCO (1950–81), and those on the New Testament by M. D. Gibson (1911–13).

All these works contain a considerable amount of material in common, and they all serve as repositories for earlier exegetical tradition.

The chief Syrian Orthodox commentators of note from the ninth century are John of Dara and, especially, Moshe bar Kepha, several of whose commentaries on different books of the Old and New Testaments survive. Only the Commentary on John by Moshe has been published in full so far.

In the first half of the eleventh century the East Syrian scholar Abdallah ibn at-Tayyib (d. 1043) wrote a number of biblical commentaries in Arabic, based largely on the earlier Syriac commentary tradition. These were widely read by Arabic-speaking Christians from all Churches, and their influence has even reached the Ethiopian commentary tradition.

An extensive commentary on the East Syrian lectionary, called the *Gannat Bussame* (*Garden of Delights*), belongs to the early thirteenth century. This work preserves many excerpts from earlier commentators whose works are otherwise lost. (An edition by G. Reinink in the CSCO is in the course of publication.)

A fitting climax to the West Syrian commentary tradition is provided by the *Awsar Raze*, or *Storehouse of Mysteries*, by the Syrian Orthodox polymath Gregory Abu'l Faraj, usually known as Bar Hebraeus (died 1286). This great work covers the entire Syriac Bible. The entire text has recently been published by the late Syrian Orthodox metropolitan of Middle Europe, Mor Julius Çiçek; only parts are available so far in English translation, namely Genesis to Samuel (M. Sprengling and W. O. Graham, 1931), and the Gospels (E. W. Carr, 1925).

CHAPTER VI

THE USE OF THE SYRIAC BIBLE IN PREACHING

The Bible has always been the main starting point for preaching in all Christian traditions. Here we shall concentrate on some features which are characteristic of the Syriac tradition and which are not found widely elsewhere.

The place of poetry has always been very prominent within Syriac literature as a whole; it is thus not surprising to find that poetry plays an important role in preaching and in the exposition of the Bible in the Syriac Churches. Two areas are particularly noteworthy: the use of dialogue poems, with biblical characters, in order to highlight decisive moments within the biblical narrative; and the use of verse homilies for the purpose of retelling biblical episodes in a dramatic fashion. Both of these may be seen as excellent vehicles for popular catechetical instruction which deserve to be revived today.

The dialogue poems belong to a very ancient literary genre which can be traced back at least to the second millennium BC. In their Syriac form these poems consist of short stanzas where the two biblical characters speak in alternating verses; there is almost always a short narrative introduction, providing the audience (the congregation) with the biblical setting, and there is sometimes a very brief conclusion (often in the form of a doxology). The poems normally take the form of an argument between the two biblical characters, and in the end one of the two speakers wins over the other. Thus, for example, in the dialogue between the angel Gabriel and the Virgin Mary (the scene of the Annunciation, Luke 1:26–38), the Virgin is mindful of Eve's experience, and so questions the angel at first:

> The angel addressed the Virgin and said,
> Peace be with you, O mother of my Lord,
> blessed are you, child,
> and blessed is the Fruit that is within you.

> And Mary says, Who are you, sir?
> and what is this that you utter?
> What you are saying is remote from me,
> and what it means I have no idea.

Angel   The Father has revealed to me, as I do now to you,
> this mystery which is shared between him and his Son,
> when he sent me to say
> that from you he will shine out over the worlds.

Mary   I am afraid, sir, to accept you,
> for when Eve my mother accepted the serpent
> who spoke as her friend,
> she was snatched away from her former glory.

Human experience and the dictates of reason also provide a basis for further questioning on Mary's part:

Mary   This meeting with you and your presence here
> are all very fine, if only the natural order of things
> did not stir me to have doubts at your arrival
> as to how there can be fruit in a virgin's womb.

It is only when the angel finally mentions the Holy Spirit that Mary finally accepts:

Angel   I was sent from the Father to bring you this message,
> that his love has compelled him
> so that his Son should reside in your womb,
> and over you the Holy Spirit will reside.

Mary   In that case, O angel, I will not answer back:
> if the Holy Spirit shall come to me,
> I am his maidservant, and he has authority;
> let it be to me in accordance with your word.

These dialogue poems provide a very effective means of pin-pointing moments of dramatic tension within the biblical narrative. At each such dramatic point the poet (usually anonymous) explores the inner psychological tensions and thoughts; in the process of doing so, he successfully brings out the important underlying theological teaching of the passage in question. In many cases these poems deal with the conflict between the head and the heart, between human reason and faith: we have seen a little of this in the dialogue between the Angel and Mary, but it is also very prominent in the dialogues between Zechariah and the Angel, and between Joseph and Mary. Zechariah finds it impossible to believe the angel's message that his barren and elderly wife will bear a son: he tells the angel "It would be astonishing if I were to believe you in the matter of this tale which I you have told me: a tree already dried up cannot possibly provide fruit." In vain does the angel tell Zechariah of the Old Testament precedents, such as Sarah giving birth to Isaac in her old age; Zechariah remains stubbornly sceptical: "However much you speak trying to persuade me, your words still do not touch my intellect." In Zechariah's case human reason proves the victor over faith—with the result that Zechariah was made "unable to speak until the angel's words came to pass."

In the case of Joseph, on the other hand, faith eventually wins the day, even though external appearances—his fiancée's obvious pregnancy—make it very hard for him to believe in Mary's improbable explanation, as appears near the beginning of the dialogue:

> Joseph   I am astounded at what you say:
> how can I listen to your words?
> Virgins simply do not get pregnant
> unless they have intercourse or get married.

Mary's patience in the face of his angry disbelief eventually, towards the end of the long dialogue, wins over Joseph, and he half concedes that Mary might be telling the truth:

> Joseph   There are two possibilities, and both disturb me:
> if what you say is true, it is most frightening for me,
> but if it is untrue, that is a great grief.
> How I wish I could escape from the two.

To this Mary replies:

> Now I shall pour out my words
> and address my Son hidden within my womb;
> he will reveal to you that I shall have no other children,
> and that I shall not be deprived of your company.

This is the final verse of the dialogue, but in the final narrative we hear that verification of the truth of Mary's words is provided for Joseph:

> Joseph slept, and the angel arrived,
> revealing to him how the mystery had taken place.
> Joseph rose up early and knelt in worship before Mary
> full of wonder, who had not lied.

The dialogue poem between Mary and Joseph illustrates how it is only after the intellect has given way to the improbable claims of faith that external verification if provided (in Joseph's case, in the dream), showing that this faith is indeed grounded in reality.

Some fifty such dialogue poems survive, and the majority of these involve biblical characters. Based on the Old Testament we have: Cain and Abel (Gen 4), Abraham and Isaac (Gen 22), Joseph and Potiphar's wife (Gen 39), Joseph and Benjamin, and Job and his wife. The dialogues with New Testament topics are rather more numerous, and include: Zechariah and the Angel, the Angel and Mary, Joseph and Mary, Mary and the Magi, John the Baptist and Christ, John the Baptist and the Crowd, Christ and the Pharisees, Christ and the Synagogue, the Sinful Woman and Satan, the two thieves on the cross, the Cherub and the thief (Luke 22:42–3), Death and Satan (at the descent of Christ into Sheol), and Mary and the Gardener (the risen Christ).

The oldest dialogue poems are by none other than St. Ephrem (some on Death and Satan); most of these poems, however, are anonymous, though in the East Syrian tradition they have usually been ascribed to Narsai. Probably many of them will have been written in the fifth or sixth centuries, for this was a period of great literary creativity. But later writers also continued to use this form of dialogue poetry to good effect.

Syriac literature is extremely rich in verse homilies, and many of these are by the great poets Ephrem (d. 373), Narsai (d. ca. 500), and Jacob of Serugh (d. 521). A large number of these homilies provide sermons in verse on particular biblical passages, exploring their spiritual meanings, making creative use of typology. In these the readers (or hearers) are always aware of the preacher himself standing between them and the biblical text, providing exhortations and explanations. There is, however, also a smaller number of verse homilies where the biblical narrative is retold in dramatic fashion; in these there are no homiletic asides. This retelling of biblical narratives makes ample use of speeches by the various biblical characters involved; some of these speeches can already be found, in very brief form, in the biblical text itself. But more often the poet has supplied both the occasion as well as the words; in so doing he is reading between the lines, as it were, of the biblical text, and drawing out the dramatic potential to be found there.

Once again, most of the narrative poems of this sort are anonymous (though they are often wrongly attributed to Ephrem). It seems likely that they mostly belong to the fifth and sixth centuries. Among the subjects covered we find the following: Abraham and Sarah in Egypt (Gen 12), Abraham, Sarah, and Isaac (Gen 22), Joseph and his brothers (Gen 37–48; the long cycle of poems on this subject by the fifth century poet Balai is often wrongly ascribed to Ephrem), the prophet Elijah and the widow of Sarephta (1 Kings 17), the prophet Jonah (this alone is for certain genuinely by Ephrem), Mary and Joseph (making use of motifs in the Proto-Gospel of James), and the Sinful Woman who anointed the feet of Christ, which might possibly also be genuine Ephrem (Luke 7:36–50 and parallels).

The two narrative poems retelling the episode of the sacrifice of Isaac are of particular interest since they introduce the figure of Sarah, who is not mentioned a single time in the course of the biblical text of Genesis 22. In retelling the biblical narrative the poet seeks to explore the silences of the actual text of the Bible, and to draw out what could be implicit within those silences. What were Sarah's reactions when Abraham took off her young boy? Did Abraham tell her of God's fearful command? Preachers in the early Church were clearly intensely concerned with such questions, and they suggested a variety of possible answers. Usually they assume that she only let Isaac go because she was unaware of what Abraham had been instructed by God to do. In one of the two Syriac narrative poems on the subject, however, we have a quite different approach: Sarah is portrayed as having the same profound faith in God's ultimate love as her husband Abraham has, for she is both aware of what is to happen and consents to it. Indeed, as it turns out, her faith proves even greater than Abraham's, for she has to endure the testing of her faith twice: when Abraham and Isaac return home to her, Abraham at first goes in alone, saying to Isaac "I will spy out your mother's mind." Sarah is thus left to imagine that Isaac has indeed been sacrificed, and she welcomes her husband back with these words:

> Welcome, blessed old man, husband who has loved God;
> welcome, happy one, who has sacrificed on the pyre my only child;
> welcome, o slaughterer, who did not spare the body of my only child.
> Did he weep when he was bound, or groan when he died?
> Was he looking for me?

Abraham assures her that Isaac did not cry when he was bound, and that "when the knife was above his throat, he remembered you there." To this Sarah replies:

> May the soul of my only child be accepted,
> for he listened to his mother's words.
> If only I were an eagle, or had the speed of a dove,
> so that I might go and behold that place
> where my only child, my beloved, was sacrificed!

Only at the end of this speech does Isaac walk in, safe and sound, to fall into his mother's astounded embrace.

Although the poet handles the biblical narrative with a good deal of freedom, he does so in order to impress on his readers and hearers the underlying message inherent in the biblical text; this he does by means of various dramatic effects which he introduces into the retelling of the biblical story. We should not, of course, suppose that he is trying to provide a historical reconstruction of the episode: this would be to misunderstand his intentions totally and completely.

The narrative verse homily on the prophet Elijah provides another example of the way in which the poet seeks to heighten the dramatic force of the biblical narrative. 1 Kings 17:1 tells how the prophet bound the skies under an oath, not allowing them to let fall any rain or dew "except by my word." The resulting drought was to be a punishment for the nation's wicked ways. Later on in the chapter the biblical narrative tells how the same prophet restored life to the dead son of the Widow at Sarepta (1 Kings 17:22). Then, at the end of chapter eighteen, we learn of the end of the terrible drought. In the biblical account no direct connection between the raising of the widow's son and the end of the drought is made, but the author of the Syriac verse homily on Elijah does link the two in a very dramatic way (in so doing, he was in fact following Jewish tradition). When the heavens complain to God about Elijah's action, God points out to them that he should respect his prophet's authority, seeing that Elijah had specifically stated that the heavens were bound until he himself release them. "Be patient with me for a little while," God tells the heavens, "and wait until I go down to visit him. I will go on proposing to him reasons, until he eventually becomes reconciled with you." After various attempts to get Elijah to lift his ban and so end the drought, God finally sends him off to a widow of Sarepta who will feed him despite the famine. She tells him that all she has left over is a little flour in a bowl and a small quantity of oil (1 Kings 17:12), but the prophet assures her:

> Neither shall the bowl of flour fail
> nor shall the horn of oil give out.

The women runs off "to try out the word of the prophet," and as "she plunged her hand into the bowl, flour came leaping up to meet it"—and the same thing happened with the oil. The prophet, the widow, and her son are thus assured of food, and all goes well for a while. But the drought and the famine continue, since Elijah has not yet lifted his ban. Things are getting so bad that God decides to resort to something more dramatic in order to get Elijah to relent and show compassion:

He sent an angel to take away
the soul of the widow's son.
He took away his soul, and so incited his mother
to do battle with the upright man:
the woman took hold of him and stood there,
ready to argue with him as a murderer.
"Give me back my only child," she cried,
"for he was killed because of you.
I will seize hold of you straightaway
and throw you into the hands
of Ahab and Jezebel, to meet an evil fate."
Elijah answered her and said
to the widow who had spoken these things:
"Never has anyone been killed by me,
and here you are calling me a murderer.
Am I God, to be able to revive your son?
Or is his soul in my hands,
seeing that you are requiring him at my hands?"

The woman said in reply to Elijah,
"Indeed, by the God whom I serve,
this is assured for me:
if the flour heard you and leapt up,
and if the oil heard you and spurted forth,
then the Lord will listen to you thus
and will give you back the soul of the boy."

Then Elijah took the boy
and brought him to the upper room;
he knelt and began to say
in sorrow and in suffering,
"O Lord, I beg of you,
as a servant I speak in your presence;
why, Lord, have you repaid with such loss
this widow who has received me?
Why did you send me to her,
why did you bring her son forth from her womb?
Lord, I call upon you with feeling,
I beg of you mercy;
listen, Lord, to your servant's prayer,
and return the soul of this boy."
Our Lord answered and said to Elijah,
"You owe me one debt:
repay it, and I will listen to you.

In your hands is placed the key to the heavens,
in my hands is the soul of the child."
The holy man opened his mouth
as his heart rejoiced and exulted;
he released the heavens which he had bound
—and the soul of the child returned.

In order to heighten the dramatic effect of the biblical narrative the poet has introduced the bold idea of a bargain struck between God and Elijah. This has the effect of emphasizing the double underlying message which the poet sees in the biblical narrative: the need for compassion on the part of those who are zealous for God's righteousness, and the example of the widow's faith in God's ability to work miracles through his prophet.

By retelling the biblical narrative in a lively and imaginative way, these anonymous Syriac poets have provided a very effective form of popular preaching. The very fact that they take some liberties with the biblical text encourages their readers and hearers to go back to the biblical text and re-discover it for themselves.

CHAPTER VII

THE USE OF THE SYRIAC BIBLE IN THE LITURGY

The Syriac Bible features in liturgical worship above all in the cycle of biblical readings and in the use of the Psalms. Here, however, we shall consider another aspect: the way in which the phraseology of the Syriac Bible is ingrained in the very prayers and hymns of the Syriac Churches. We shall look at two examples, based on Genesis 1:2 and on Luke 1:35.

The second half of Genesis 1:2 reads in the Peshitta "and the Spirit of God was hovering (*mraḥḥefa*) over the surface of the water." The verb *raḥḥef* is used in Deuteronomy 32:11 of a female bird hovering over her chicks, and the noun *mraḥfana* is found several times in the Peshitta as a parallel to *mraḥmana*, "compassionate." Modern English translations usually provide two possible alternative translations for Genesis 1:2, "the Spirit of God" and "wind of God" (or, "strong wind"), since *ruaḥ* in Hebrew (and *ruḥa* in Syriac) can mean either "spirit" or "wind." This hesitation on the part of modern translators is in fact nothing new, for the early Church Fathers were also divided over how to interpret the verse: does it refer to the Holy Spirit, or to a spirit/wind? The fact that the Greek has a passive verb following ("was carried") suggested to some Greek commentators that "the spirit" here could not refer to the Holy Spirit.

The Syriac Fathers share this uncertainty over the interpretation of Genesis 1:2, and many of them, from St. Ephrem onwards, prefer not to introduce the Holy Spirit here in their exegesis of the passage. This line of interpretation was adopted in order to avoid certain theological misunderstandings associated with the verse, and it was followed by several later commentators, and in particular by Theodore of Mopsuestia, from whom it was taken over by the School of Edessa and by its successor at Nisibis. Accordingly, the vast majority of later Syriac commentaries, especially those in the East Syrian tradition, take the view that the "spirit of God" in the verse is not the Holy Spirit.

Nevertheless, in spite of this attitude on the part of some theologians, it seems that a different understanding was deeply ingrained in the liturgical tradition, for there we can find many passages where Genesis 1:2 is understood as referring to the Holy Spirit. This can be seen above all in prayers and hymns connected with baptism; here we often find a parallelism drawn between the creative activity of the Holy Spirit over the primordial waters, on the one hand, and the same creative activity of the Spirit over the baptismal waters, where the baptized become a "new creation." Thus in one of the Epiphany Hymns attributed to St. Ephrem we have:

> At creation the Spirit hovered over the waters;
> they conceived and gave birth to reptiles, fish and birds.
> The Holy Spirit has hovered over the baptismal water, and has given
> birth to eagles in symbol, that is, to the virgins and leaders ,
> and to fishes in symbol, that is, to the chaste and the intercessors,
> and to reptiles in symbol, that is, to the cunning who have become as
> simple as doves (Matthew 10:16).

> (Hymns on Epiphany 8:15)

The same idea is also found in the Maronite baptismal rite, in the course of the long prayer at the sanctification of the water:

> As the Holy Spirit hovered over the waters at the establishment of
> creation, so may your Holy Spirit, O Lord, hover over this baptismal
> water which is a spiritual womb, and may he rest upon it and sanctify it
> and make it fruitful with the heavenly Adam, in place of the earthly
> Adam.

The parallelism between the waters at creation and the baptismal water is richly suggestive, but it is rarely brought out in an explicit way—perhaps as a result of the different exegeses of Genesis 1:2 which dominated the Schools of Edessa and Nisibis. But very often we do find the parallelism vestigially present, thanks to the use of the verb *rahhef* in connection with the activity of the Spirit at baptism. Thus St. Ephrem, who specifically does not take the "spirit of God" to refer to the Holy Spirit, nevertheless does use the verb *rahhef*, "hover," with reference to baptism when he says "The Holy Spirit hovers over the streams" (that is, of the baptismal waters) [Hymns on Virginity 7:8]. Likewise, in some texts of the Syrian Orthodox baptismal service the deacon says at the sanctification of the baptismal water, "How fearful is this hour when the living and Holy Spirit circles down from the uppermost heights and hovers and dwells on the water, sanctifying it, just as the Jordan's streams were sanctified [at the baptism of Christ]."

Likewise, outside the context of baptism and the baptismal liturgy, we not infrequently find the Spirit described as "hovering," where the verb "hover" is derived from the Peshitta text of Genesis 1:2. Thus in several West Syrian Anaphoras "hover" is used as one of the verbs describing the activity of the Holy Spirit at the Epiclesis. One such case is the Syriac Anaphora ascribed to St John Chrysostom (quite different from the Greek Anaphora under his name):

> May your Spirit and your Power overshadow this holy altar and sanctify its offerings; and may He hover and rest and reside over the bread, and may it become one Body…

The wording of this particular epiclesis conveniently introduces us to the other biblical passage under consideration in this section, for the verb "overshadow" is derived from Luke 1:35, "The Holy Spirit shall come and the Power of the Most High shall overshadow (*naggen*) you."

The Syriac verb used to translate the Greek word here for "overshadow" is a very interesting one, for it has a background in Jewish Aramaic. The verb *aggen* occurs a number of times in the Jewish Aramaic translations of the Hebrew Bible, almost always in the context of God's salvific activity. The Syriac translators of the New Testament evidently inherited the term from Jewish Aramaic and used it in a number of different passages, including Luke 1:35. Among the other passages where the translators employed this verb *aggen* are John 1:14 (where the Greek has "The Word dwelt, or tabernacled, among us") and Acts 10:44 and 11:15 (where the Greek has "the Spirit fell upon…").

As was the case with Genesis 1:2, so too with Luke 1:35 there has been a difference of opinion about its precise interpretation. Is "the Power of the Most High" the same as "the Holy Spirit" earlier in the verse, or is the Power to be identified as the divine Word? On the whole one can say that East Syrian exegetical tradition identified the Power as a synonym for the Holy Spirit, while West Syrian tradition normally understood "the Power of the Most High" to refer to the pre-existent Word; several exceptions can, however, be found to this pattern of interpretation in both traditions. In the case of the West Syrian tradition it is clear that the Peshitta's use of the same verb, *aggen*, at John 1:14 has been influential, for there the Word is subject of the verb.

In view of this difference over the interpretation of Luke 1:35, one would expect to find reminiscences of Luke 1:35, where the Holy Spirit is understood to be the subject of the verb "overshadow," only in East Syrian liturgical texts, and not in West Syrian ones. This, however, is not the case, and in fact we find many such reminiscences in both liturgical traditions.

It is particularly significant when reminiscences of Luke 1:35 occur in the Epiclesis of the Eucharistic Liturgy. In the East Syrian liturgical tradition this occurs in the East Syrian Anaphora of Theodore, where the invocation opens with the words "May the grace of the Holy Spirit come upon us and upon this offering and reside in and overshadow this bread..." In West Syrian Anaphoras the use of "overshadow" in the epiclesis is especially common, and the example quoted above, from the Anaphora of St John Chrysostom, is only one out of many Anaphoras where "overshadow" is used at this point.

The use of the word "overshadow" in the epiclesis deliberately draws attention to the important parallelism between the activity of the Spirit over Mary and the activity of the Spirit over the eucharistic Offerings. In his Commentary on the Liturgy the Syrian Orthodox writer Moshe bar Kepha says

> Just as the Holy Spirit descended to the womb of Mary (as the angel said, "for the Holy Spirit shall come..."), and made the body of God the Word from the flesh of the Virgin, so too the Spirit descends on the bread and wine on the altar and makes them into the Body and the Blood of God the Word which originated from the Virgin.

The implications of this implicit parallelism between the Annunciation and the Eucharist are important. At the Annunciation Mary's willing co-operation with the Spirit resulted in the birth from her of God the Word; at the Eucharist there are two different aspects of the activity of the Spirit: firstly, through the Church's faithful co-operation with the Holy Spirit at the Epiclesis, the eucharistic Offerings are transformed and become the Body and Blood of Christ; secondly, if those who receive Communion imitate Mary's willing co-operation with the Holy Spirit, they too will give birth spiritually to God the Word. Thus the eighth-century East Syrian mystic, Joseph the Visionary, writes in a prayer to be recited before Communion, "May I receive you, Lord, not into the stomach which belongs to the body's limbs, but into the womb of my mind, so that you may be conceived there, as in the womb of the Virgin."

Syriac liturgical texts are full of such biblical reminiscences, and the theological richness of these texts will only become truly apparent when these reminiscences and allusions are recognized. Sometimes these allusions refer to wording which is found uniquely in the Peshitta (this applies to some extent, at least, to the two examples quoted above; it also applies notably to the form of the Sanctus in the Syriac liturgies, for the wording "heaven and earth are full of his praises" (rather than "his glory") is taken from the Peshitta text of Isaiah 6:3. Because Syriac liturgical prayers and hymns are so soaked in the phraseology of the Syriac Bible, we can accordingly see the importance of having translations based on the Peshitta for the purposes of liturgical readings from the Bible.

CHAPTER VIII

THE PESHITTA AS THE BASIS FOR SYRIAC SPIRITUALITY

The Peshitta is the source for a great many terms which were to become important in the history of the Syriac spirituality. Before looking at a few of these in more detail, we can notice the following in passing:

- The term "*rushma*," or "*mark*," is regularly used in early Syriac literature for the baptismal anointing on the forehead (or, by extension, it may also refer to the whole baptismal rite). The source for the term is the Peshitta text of Ezekiel 9:4, where the prophet Ezekiel has a vision of the slaughter of the guilty in Jerusalem; in this vision "a man clothed in linen," evidently an angelic being, is told by God to pass through the city of Jerusalem and "put a mark ("*rushma*") on the foreheads of those who groan in torment over all the abominations and evil doings that are being performed in the city." In Hebrew the work for "*mark*" here is "*taw*," the letter T, whose shape in the old Hebrew script was that of a cross. At the pre-baptismal anointing the priest anoints a cross on the forehead of the person being baptized with oil, which symbolizes (among many other things) protection against the forces of evil.

- In East Syrian writers like St. Isaac of Nineveh (seventh century) the concept of "pure prayer" becomes a very important one. The only biblical version where the actual term "pure prayer" occurs is the Peshitta, at 1 Chronicles 16:42: "These holy men (who were ministering before the Ark of the Covenant) gave praise, not with musical instruments of praise, ... but with a joyful mouth and with pure and perfect prayer."

- One of the central concepts of Syriac spirituality is the ideal of *shafyutha*; the Syriac term has no single English equivalent, but covers a whole variety of different ideas, such as "lucidity, luminosity, purity, clarity, serenity." In the Syriac Bible there are a number of important passages where the adjective *shafya*, "clear,

99

luminous," et cetera, occurs; in some of these the term is used to describe a path or way, such as Isaiah 26:7, "Straight and clear (*shafya*) is the way of the righteous." But the most important passage is Luke 8:15, where the term is associated with the heart: "The seed in the good ground refers to those who hear the Word with a luminous (*shafya*) and good heart" (the Greek has "an excellent and good heart"). Taking this as their starting point, later Syriac writers frequently refer to the ideal of *shafyut lebba*, "luminosity of heart."

• Another important and distinctive term in the history of Syriac spirituality is *msarrquta* "self-emptying"; this is used both in the sense of the stripping away of external possession, and in an interior sense, "the self-emptying of heart," the stripping away of self-will in order to follow the will of Christ. Such "self-emptying" is in fact an imitation of Christ's own self-emptying, based on St. Paul's letter to the Philippians 2:7, "Christ emptied (*sarreq*) himself, taking the form of a servant."

• Syriac tradition makes great use of the imagery of clothing in expressing many different theological ideas. In particular, the theme of the "robe, or garment, of glory/praise" is commonly used to describe the whole course of salvation history: in Paradise Adam and Eve were clothed in the garment of glory before their disobedience to God's command. At the Fall humanity lost this garment, and the whole purpose of the Incarnation was to make it possible for humanity to put on, once again, this garment of glory; to bring this about, God the Word "put on the body" at the incarnation, and then, at his Baptism in the river Jordan, he places the garment of glory in the Jordan water, ready for the individual Christian to put on at his or her baptism in the baptismal water. In this world the baptized possess this garment of glory in potential, but it only becomes a reality in the world to come—provided they have kept the garment unsullied by sin in the present life. The image of the robe or garment of glory thus links together all the main points in salvation history, and thus vividly brings home the close relationship between the individual Christian today and these past events in salvation history. Earliest Syriac Christianity evidently took the idea of Adam and Eve being clothed in Paradise with the robe of glory from an early Jewish interpretation of Genesis 3:21 (the phrase does not occur in the Peshitta text of that

passage): although the Hebrew, Greek, and Syriac texts there speak
of "garments of skin" being provided for Adam and Eve, the
Jewish Aramaic translation, known as the Targum, interprets them
as "garments of honour/glory"; similarly, a famous Rabbi, Rabbi
Meir, is said to have had a Hebrew text which read "garments of
light ('*or*)," instead of "garments of skin ('*or*)." According to this
interpretation these garments of glory or light belonged to Adam
and Eve *before* the Fall, whereas, according to the normal
translation, "garments of skin," were given to them *after* the Fall
(the Hebrew text could be interpreted either way, as far as the point
in time is concerned). Although the Syriac translators of the
Peshitta did not introduce this idea at Genesis 3:21, they do allude
to it in some other passages; thus at Psalm 8:6 the Peshitta has
"you (God) created man a little less than the angels; in honor and
glory did you 'clothe' him" (the Hebrew and the Greek both have
"crown him," not "clothe him"). Likewise at Psalm 132:16 the
Peshitta (but not the Hebrew and Greek) speaks of "glory" as the
clothing of the just. In the Peshitta New Testament the translators
have introduced the idea of the Incarnation as "putting on the
body" at two places in the Letter to the Hebrews; at Hebrews 5:7
Christ is described as "being clothed in flesh" (the Greek has "in
the days of his flesh"); and at Hebrews 10:5 (where Psalm 40 is
quoted as a prophecy of Christ) the Syriac has "You clothed me in
a body," whereas the Greek has "You prepared a body for me."

• We have already seen the importance of the term "*aggen*" (based
especially on Luke 1:35 and John 1:14) in the Syriac liturgical
tradition. In some later Syriac writers (notably St. Isaac of Nineveh)
the term also became an important one for describing the
transforming action of the Holy Spirit on the interior "altar of the
heart."

All these terms are based on some distinctive feature to be found only
in the Syriac Bible. There are, of course, many other biblical terms which
are likewise characteristic of Syriac spirituality, but these are also to be
found in the Greek and Hebrew, as well as in the Syriac Bible.

Further information on this subject can be found in my *Spirituality in
the Syriac Tradition* (Moran 'Etho 2, 1989; 2nd edn 2005).

PART II:
THE SYRIAC BIBLE

THE BIBLE IN SYRIAC[1]

Amongst the translations of the Bible made in antiquity those into Syriac play an important role. Although there is a single official translation of the Bible for all the Syriac Churches, known as the Peshitta (Peshito), a number of other translations or revisions are preserved.

A BIRD'S EYE VIEW OF THE SYRIAC TRANSLATIONS OF THE BIBLE

The Old Testament

For the Old Testament the oldest version, the Peshitta, has always been the standard version of the Syriac Churches; this was made directly from the Hebrew original, and it is likely that it should be dated to the second century AD. Since this is by far the most important and influential of the Syriac translations, it will receive special attention further on.

But beside the Peshitta there are three later translations, based on the Greek text of the Septuagint, a translation which goes back to the third and second century BC; these later translations into Syriac were carried out in the period between the sixth and early eighth century. The earliest of these is only known from a fragmentary manuscript of Isaiah, and it is likely that this was a translation commissioned by Philoxenos (d. 523), bishop of Mabbugh, who also commissioned a revision of the Peshitta New Testament. The second is Paul of Tella's complete translation of the revised Septuagint column in the massive comparative edition, known as the Hexapla, which had been undertaken by the great scholar Origen in the early third century. Because of this origin, the translation has been given the name of "Syrohexapla" by Western scholars, while in Syriac writers it is

---

[1] Originally published (without the footnotes) as Chapter IX of vol. III of *The Hidden Pearl: The Syrian Orthodox Church and its Ancient Aramaic Heritage* (Rome, 2001). Some basic annotation was provided separately in *Hugoye* 5:1 (2002), and this, in an updated form, constitutes the basis of the footnotes here.

simply known as "the Seventy" (referring to its origin in the Greek Septuagint). The third of the later translations is not so much a completely new translation, but rather, a revision of the Peshitta, on the basis of some Greek manuscripts of the Septuagint, undertaken by Jacob of Edessa right at the end of his life. Jacob's revision, however, only covered a few books of the Old Testament.

At a very much later date, probably in the seventeenth century, Syriac translations of certain books of the Latin Vulgate were produced in India. This will almost certainly have been done at the instigation of European missionaries, who were suspicious of the Syriac texts traditionally used by Christians of the Syriac Church in southern India. In the Middle East some other books of the Vulgate Old Testament got translated into Syriac, though not always directly; thus in 1818 the priest Petros Asmar of Tel Kephe (Iraq) translated 1–3 Maccabees and various other books into Syriac from an Arabic version that itself derived from the Vulgate.

Even more recently, in the latter part of the nineteenth century, a revision of the Peshitta Psalter was made by Joseph David and published in Mosul in 1877 (he was subsequently appointed Syrian Catholic archbishop of Damascus). This revision, which is described further below (under The Psalter), brought the Peshitta text here and there into closer line with the Hebrew.

The New Testament

For the New Testament, the earliest translation into Syriac seems to have been a harmony of the four Gospels, known as the Diatessaron and compiled by Tatian a little after the middle of the second century AD. This was the Gospel text commented on by Ephrem in the fourth century, but it subsequently fell out of use and disappeared. The earliest surviving Gospel text in Syriac, known as the Old Syriac, was perhaps translated in the early third century and is preserved in two very early manuscripts, both of the fifth century. During the course of the fourth century the Old Syriac seems to have been sporadically revised, and one of these revisions came to be very widely circulated, and so became the official translation, known as the Peshitta, for all the Syriac Churches. The widespread adoption of this revision must have taken place around 400 AD. The Peshitta also includes Acts, the Pauline Epistles, and the three major Catholic Epistles, James, 1 Peter, and 1 John; evidently the New Testament canon of the early Syriac Churches was restricted to these books, and it was only in the sixth century that the other Catholic Epistles, 2 Peter, 2–3 John and Jude, and Revelation, were first translated into Syriac. Possibly connected with these translations, a revision of the Peshitta, bringing it closer in line with the Greek, was commissioned by Philoxenos and undertaken by the chorepiskopos Polycarp, who completed his work in 507/8. This "Philoxenian" revision is unfortunately lost, and is only known indirectly, through the further revision made around 615 by Thomas of Harkel, and known as the Harklean.

TABLE 1:

The Place of Syriac among the Early Translations of the Bible

	From the Hebrew Old Testament	From the Greek Old Testament	From the Greek New Testament
3rd cent. BC	Greek (Septuagint, LXX)		
1st cent. BC – 2nd cent. AD	Revisions of Septuagint (Theodoton, Aquila, Symmachus)		
2nd cent. AD	**PESHITTA**	Old Latin	Old Latin
2nd/3rd cent.			**OLD SYRIAC**
2nd cent. – ca. 8th cent.	Jewish Targumim		
3rd cent.	Origen's "hexaplaric" revision of LXX		
3rd/4th cent.		Coptic	Coptic
ca. 400	Vulgate (Latin)		Vulgate
			PESHITTA
		Ethiopic	Ethiopic
			Gothic
5th cent.		Armenian	Armenian
5th/6th cent.		Georgian	Georgian
		Christian Palestinian Aramaic	Christian Palestinian Aramaic
6th cent.		**PHILOXENIAN** (Isaiah)	**PHILOXENIAN** (lost)
			ANONYMOUS, Minor Catholic Epistles and Revelation
ca. 615		**SYROHEXAPLA** ("Seventy")	**HARKLEAN**
ca. 700		**JACOB of EDESSA's** revision (select books)	

Why Is The Syriac Bible Important?

Just as many generations of English writers have been nurtured on the language of the King James Version, so too Syriac writers of all periods have been brought up on the Peshitta Bible, and this has had a profound influence on both their language and their style. Syriac poetry in particular is often deeply imbued with allusions to the Syriac Bible, and this does not apply only to liturgical poetry. This means that anyone who wants to appreciate to the full a major poet like Ephrem will need to have the same familiarity with the Syriac Bible that Ephrem expected his readers and listeners to have.

In shaping the language and terminology of liturgical texts and monastic writing, the role of the Syriac Bible has been fundamental. Here, several of the standard terms in regular use derive from phraseology that is specific to the Syriac Bible. Only in the Syriac Bible will one find phrases such as "Pure Prayer" (1 Chronicles 16:42), or "New World, New Age" (Matthew 18:28, translating "rebirth" in the Greek text), or "New Life" (Romans 6:4, rendering "newness of life" in Greek).

For the student of the Bible in general, too, there are three aspects in particular make these Syriac translations of interest.

In the first place, Syriac provides the only early version of the Gospels which is in a Semitic language. Although all the Gospels were all written in Greek, they incorporate material which will first have circulated in oral tradition in Palestinian Aramaic. The process of translating the Greek Gospels into Syriac, a different dialect of Aramaic, can on occasion throw light on what must have been the original Aramaic term used. Thus in the Lord's Prayer, Matthew has "forgive us our debts," whereas Luke provides "forgive us our sins." The Syriac versions of Matthew 6:12 all translate by *hawbayn*, literally "our debts," but also having the meaning of "wrongdoings, sins." The corresponding Palestinian Aramaic form of this word was undoubtedly the term actually used by Jesus. Even though the Syriac Gospels are translated solely from Greek, they may fortuitously recreate a word play that was very probably present in the underlying Palestinian Aramaic form of the saying. At Matthew 10:30 (and the parallel in Luke 12:7) there is no word play at all in the Greek for the phrase "all the hairs of your head are numbered," but when translated into Syriac an alliteration reappears, with *mene* corresponding to "hairs," and *manyon* to "are numbered."

Secondly, there is an exceptionally large number of very early, and well preserved, manuscripts of different parts of the Syriac Bible. Indeed, Syriac has the distinction of having the oldest dated biblical manuscript in any language, written in 459/60,[2] and a comparatively large number of Syriac biblical manuscripts belonging to the sixth century. This contrasts markedly with some of the other ancient translations, such as the Jewish Aramaic Targumim, or the Ethiopic version, where all the surviving manuscripts are very much later in date.

Thirdly, the different Syriac translations are often of considerable interest for the early history of the biblical text. In the Old Testament, the Syriac translation is one of the earliest witnesses to the standardized Hebrew text that is found in the medieval Hebrew manuscripts. As will be seen below, two other important examples of this aspect concern the New Testament.

The Origins Of The Peshitta Old Testament

Syriac scholars of the Middle Ages offered a number of different views about the origin of the standard version of the Syriac Old Testament, known from at least the ninth century as the "Peshitta/Peshito."[3] Some optimistically allocated it to the time of Solomon (supposedly at the request of king Hiram of Tyre); others placed it several centuries later, attributing it to the priest Asa, or Asya, who had been sent to Samaria by the king of Assyria (after the Assyrian conquest of the Northern Kingdom, in 721); much nearer the mark, as far as chronology was concerned, was the widespread view that it was made in the time of king Abgar and the apostle Addai.

Modern scholars are entirely in agreement that the translation was made from Hebrew, and not from Greek; on the other hand, since they have the advantage of a far wider range of evidence, it is possible for them to be more precise over the dating, and it is now widely recognized that at least most of the books of the Old Testament were translated into Syriac over the course of approximately the second century AD. Different styles of translation, and different choices of vocabulary make it certain that (as in the case of the Greek Septuagint) several different translators were at work. Since the translation was made from Hebrew, rather than from Greek, it is likely that at least the earliest translators will have been Jewish, while some of the subsequent ones may have been Christians from a Jewish background, for whom Hebrew was still familiar.

---

[2] See note 6, below.

[3] A convenient overview is given by B. ter Haar Romeny, "The Peshitta and its rivals," *The Harp* 11/12 (1999), 21–31.

In fact it is possible to identify a number of distinctive features in the Syriac Old Testament which show a knowledge of Jewish exegetical traditions. One notable case concerns the identity of the mountain upon which Noah's Ark is said to have rested at the end of the Flood (Genesis 8:4). In the Hebrew and Greek texts it is Ararat (in eastern Turkey), but in the Peshitta Old Testament and the Jewish Aramaic translations (Targumim) it is Qardu, further to the south, in the northwest of Iraq. This is a tradition that is already known to the Jewish historian Josephus, writing in the first century AD. The Syriac translation of the book of Chronicles is particularly rich in phraseology reminiscent of the Jewish Aramaic tradition (though it has no connection with the surviving Targum of Chronicles). Here, for example, one comes across several references to the Shekhina, the special term employed to denote the divine presence of God; but even more striking is the fact that, in 1 Chronicles 29:19, the Peshitta provides the earliest known attestation of one of the best known Jewish liturgical prayers, the Kaddish. The Peshitta's form of this is introduced at the end of David's prayer to God for Solomon, "O Lord my God, grant to Solomon my son a perfect heart so that he may keep Your commandments, testimonies and covenant, … so that Your great name may be sanctified and praised in the world which You created before those who fear You."

The Peshitta New Testament

The Peshitta New Testament, which represents the authorized version of all the Syriac Churches, also has a number of distinctive features: the absence of the minor Catholic Epistles and of Revelation has already been noted; the Peshitta also provides a different ordering of books, with the Letters of James, I Peter, and I John coming between Acts and the Pauline Epistles, and not after them. On occasion a different form of a place name is given, possibly reflecting an early oral tradition; thus the marriage feast to which Jesus is invited (John 3) is not at Cana, but at Qatna (which has not been successfully identified).

The Peshitta is in fact a revision of an earlier version (of which only the Gospels survive), and it was subsequently itself to be revised twice over. One might at first wonder why it was necessary to have several different Syriac translations of the New Testament, all made within a period of some 300 years. There are essentially two underlying reasons: firstly, revisions of earlier translations were thought necessary because of changing fashions in styles of translation that took place over this period; and secondly, because the earliest translations had been made from a Greek text that differed in a number of minor respects from that which emerged as the standard text from the fifth century onwards.

Why Revise Biblical Translations?

In the history of biblical translations two very different attitudes to the role of the translator can be observed: at some periods the ideal is seen to be to bring the original text to the reader, thus producing a relatively free translation; at other periods, however, it is seen as more important to bring the reader to the original, with the result that the translations are much more literal in character. The former can be described as reader-oriented, or reader-friendly, whereas the latter are essentially text-oriented. Modern translations of the Bible are almost all strongly oriented towards the reader; as a result they often contain a certain element of interpretation of the Greek original, in order to bring across the meaning more clearly. The translators of the Old Syriac Gospels likewise wished to bring the original to their readers, and one way in which they did this was to adapt Old Testament quotations in the Greek Gospels to the wording of the Syriac Old Testament, familiar to their readers. In some cases this meant that the wording of an Old Testament quotation in the Old Syriac Gospels might differ noticeably from that found in the Greek original.

A notable example of this is to be found at Luke 3:6, at the conclusion of the quotation from Isaiah 40:3–5, "The voice of one crying in the wilderness...." The end of the quotation reads in the Greek text of Luke's Gospel "and all flesh shall see the salvation of God," but in one of the Old Syriac manuscripts we find something rather different: "and the glory of the Lord shall be revealed, and all flesh shall see it together, for the mouth of the Lord has spoken"—which is exactly the wording that is to be found in the Peshitta Old Testament at Isaiah 40:5; it also happens to be a much closer translation of the Hebrew text there, in contrast to the rather free Greek translation of the Septuagint which is followed by Luke.

One of the consequences of Christianity within the Roman Empire becoming, first a recognized religion (under Constantine the Great, 306–337), and then the state religion (under Theodosius I, 379–395), was that Greek, the language of government, became more and more prestigious, at the expense of Syriac. As a result a marked shift in attitude towards the role of the translators from Greek into Syriac came about: instead of employing a comparatively free style of translation that was aimed at being reader-friendly, translators sought to reflect the Greek text of the original more accurately. This new way of thinking led to revisions being made here and there of the original Old Syriac Gospels, bringing them into closer line with the Greek. Traces of such revisions can already be seen in the two surviving manuscripts of the Old Syriac Gospels, but it was another revision, made about AD 400 and known today as the Peshitta, which was to become the official Gospel text of all the Syriac Churches.

The theological controversies of the fifth century, which led to the three-way split of the Syriac tradition led to people seeing the need for even more attention being paid to accurate translation, especially in passages around which theological controversy was focused. This new sensitivity is nicely reflected by the great Syrian Orthodox theologian, Philoxenos, writing in the early years of the sixth century. If one is concerned to translate the truth, he says, one should not be concerned to make the translation reader-friendly, by using idiomatic Syriac language; rather, it is necessary to reflect the exact terminology of the original Greek, "for what is placed in the Holy Scriptures is not the child of human thoughts, so that it should receive correction or adjustment by means of human knowledge." "It was for this reason," he goes on, "that we have now undertaken to have the Holy Scriptures translated anew from Greek into Syriac."[4]

Philoxenos is here referring to the revision of the Peshitta New Testament undertaken by his chorepiskopos Polycarp, which was completed in 508. As was noted above, Polycarp's own work does not survive in its original form, but it constituted the basis for a much more literal revision undertaken a century later, by Thomas of Harkel. Over the course of this century many remarkable advances in translation technique had been made, the aim being to reflect as many details of the Greek originals as possible. Today one often thinks of literal translations as clumsy affairs, produced by inexperienced translators. This was certainly not the case with Thomas and the other translators of his time, for their method of producing highly literal (and thus, very much text-oriented) translations was extremely sophisticated and very carefully thought out. A good example of their approach can be seen in the way they translated the angel Gabriel's greeting to Mary in Luke 1:28. The Greek text has the normal Greek word of greeting, *chaire*, traditionally translated into English as "Hail" while more recent translations have "Greetings"; in the Old Syriac and Peshitta this is rendered by the idiomatic Syriac equivalent, *shlom lekh(y)*, which literally

---

[4] Philoxenos, *Commentary on the Prologue of John* (ed. A. de Halleux, CSCO Scr. Syri 165; 1977), 53. A discussion of Philoxenos' comments can be found in my "The resolution of the Philoxenian/Harklean problem," in E. J. Epp and G. D. Fee (eds.), *New Testament Textual Criticism: Essays in Honour of B. M. Metzger* (Oxford, 1981), 325–43.

means "peace to you," but for the seventh-century school of translation this was considered inaccurate, and so the wording was altered to *hdoy*, "Rejoice," which is a literal rendering of the Greek word *chaire*.

The Syriac translators of the late sixth and the seventh centuries were by no means alone in advocating the practice of literal translation. The view that biblical translation should be literal goes back to Jerome, the translator of the Latin Vulgate, who was working at much the same time that the Peshitta revision of the Syriac New Testament was being made. Jerome's ideal for biblical translation in due course came to be extended to almost all translation in the Late Antiquity and the Middle Ages, and was applied to translations from Greek into Latin, Armenian, and Georgian, just as much as to those into Syriac. A change in practice, moving back to the Hellenistic Greek and Roman preference for reader-oriented translations, only came in the sixteenth century in Europe, with the invention of printing and the period of the Reformation.

A Developing Biblical Text

A second reason was mentioned above why revisions of the Syriac biblical text were necessary, and this concerned the fact that the underlying Greek text available by the fifth century was different in several detailed respects from the more primitive Greek text that had been used for the Old Syriac Gospels. Although this fact explains many of the differences between the Old Syriac and the Peshitta Gospels, it was probably not a prominent motivating force behind the revision, and the revisers probably will have considered these differences to be due more to the earlier translators' freedom in rendering the Greek, rather than to a different underlying Greek text. For the modern scholar, however, this aspect is of great interest, since the Greek text underlying the Old Syriac Gospels preserves some very archaic readings, some of which have almost entirely been lost in the Greek manuscript tradition. A striking example of this can be found at Matthew 27:16–17, where Pilate offers to release a prisoner, giving the crowd a choice between Barabbas and Jesus. The vast majority of Greek manuscripts and early translations have the following:

> They had then a notorious prisoner, called Barabbas. So when they had gathered, Pilate said to them, "Whom do you want me to release for you, Barabbas, or Jesus who is called Christ?"

Instead of "Barabbas," the Old Syriac has "Jesus Bar Aba," so that the crowd is being offered a choice between two men both called Jesus. It is very likely that the Old Syriac (together with a very small number of Greek manuscripts) has preserved the original reading here, and this was subsequently dropped from the text out of reverence for the name of Jesus, resulting in the reading found in all the other Greek manuscripts and early translations. The fact that Jesus and Aba were both common names in first-century Palestine simply confirms this interpretation of the evidence, and so it is not surprising to find that several authoritative modern English translations of the Bible have adopted the reading of the Old Syriac here. There is now, in fact, a double ambiguity, for "Jesus Bar Aba" could be taken as "Jesus, son of the Father," rather than "Jesus, son of Aba."

Behind The Printed Syriac Bible

Today one is used to having the whole Bible available in a single volume that is of a convenient size and easy to handle. It is easy to forget that this is in fact a comparatively modern luxury, made possible by the invention of printing. Before this, the contents of the whole Bible would normally be transmitted in quite a number of separate hand-written volumes, most of which would contain a particular group of books (such as the Gospels), though some might only contain just one book at a time. Very rarely a complete Bible (called a "Pandect") might be produced, but this would be a very expensive undertaking, and the resulting volume would be huge and unmanageable. Even if the Old and New Testaments were bound as separate volumes, the inconvenience of an unwieldy size would still apply for the Old Testament one, as can be seen from the very few such Old Testament Pandects that survive.

Which Books Are Canonical?

These practical considerations, which led to dividing up the biblical books into smaller groups, had certain important consequences. This was especially the case as far as the Old Testament is concerned, for it meant that there was no clear-cut idea of what books it contained, or in what order they might be given. Of course all the books that feature in the Hebrew Bible are regularly found, but there are certain others which are usually also treated as belonging, and others again which feature now and then in otherwise biblical manuscripts. This situation applies for the most part to books designated as "deuterocanonical" in the Roman Catholic tradition, and as "Apocrypha" in the Reformed tradition. In fact the Syriac manuscript tradition shares this lack of any fixed Old Testament canon with the Greek manuscript tradition of the Septuagint.

If one compares the contents of the four great Old Testament Pandects that survive in manuscripts older than the thirteenth century, one can readily see the different choices that have been made. Thus the famous sixth- or seventh-century manuscript in the Ambrosian Library, Milan, includes the following books: Wisdom of Solomon, Letters of Jeremiah and of Baruch, Baruch, Bel and the Dragon, Susanna, Judith, Bar Sira (Ecclesiasticus), Apocalypse of Baruch, Apocalypse of Ezra (IV Ezra), and 1–4 Maccabees. The selection in the seventh- or eighth-century illustrated Pandect in the Bibliothèque Nationale, Paris, only partly overlaps: Wisdom of Solomon, Prayer of Manasseh, Letter of Baruch, Baruch, Letter of Jeremiah, Susanna, Bel and the Dragon, Judith, Bar Sira, and I–III Maccabees. In the ninth-century Pandect in the Laurentian Library, Florence, the number of such books is reduced considerably, to: Prayer of Manasseh, Bel and the Dragon, Susanna, and Judith. The illustrated Pandect (sometimes referred to as "the Buchanan Bible") in the University Library, Cambridge, belonging to the twelfth century, reverts to a larger selection: Wisdom of Solomon, Letter of Baruch, Baruch, Letter of Jeremiah, Bel and the Dragon, Susanna, I–IV Maccabees, III Ezra, and Tobit.

It is interesting to compare the contents of these manuscripts with the two main printed Bibles which include the so-called "Apocrypha," the Mosul edition of 1887–91 and the United Bibles Societies' edition of 1979. In the former, the following books are present: (in volume I) Tobit, Judith, Esther 10:4–16:24; (in volume II) Wisdom, Bar Sira, Letter of Jeremiah, 1–2 Baruch, Susanna, Bel, 1–2 Maccabees.

For the Old Testament, the United Bible Societies' edition of the Syriac Bible simply reproduced the edition by Samuel Lee (1823), but since Lee's edition deliberately excluded the Apocrypha, the text of these was supplied as a separate section entitled "Apocrypha" (this was reproduced from the handwriting of Yuhanon Sevan). The additional books thus incorporated are exactly the same as those in the Mosul edition (which evidently served as the source which was copied), although in a different order.

All these books are translated from Greek, with the exception of Bar Sira, which was made directly from the Hebrew text, before that was lost (only in the twentieth century has most of the Hebrew original been recovered, either from the Geniza, or store room, of the medieval Jewish synagogue in Cairo, or from finds in the Judaean Desert).

This practice of copying the Old Testament in several different volumes has a second important consequence: there is no fixed sequence of books. This can again be readily observed by comparing the different orderings of the books in the four great Pandects:

TABLE 2:

Order of Books in Complete Old Testament Manuscripts

Milan	Paris	Florence	Cambridge
Pentateuch	Pentateuch	Pentateuch	Pentateuch
Job	Job	Joshua	Job
Joshua	Joshua	Judges	Joshua
Judges	Judges	1-2 Samuel	Judges
1-2 Samuel	Ruth	1-2 Kings	1-2 Samuel
Psalms	1-2 Sam.	1-2 Chron.	Psalms
1-2 Kings	1-2 Kings	Psalms	1-2 Kings
Proverbs	1-2 Chron.	Odes	1-2 Chron.
Wisdom	Prov.	Prayer of Manasseh	Proverbs
Qohelet	Qohelet	Isaiah	Qohelet
Song of Songs	Song of Songs	Jeremiah	Song of Songs
Isaiah	Wisdom	Lamentations	Wisdom
Jeremiah	Prayer of Manasseh	Ezekiel	Isaiah
Lamentations	Isaiah	XII Prophets	Jeremiah
Letter of Jeremiah	Jeremiah	Daniel	Lamentations
Letter of Baruch	Lamentations	Bel	Letter of Baruch
Baruch	Letter of Baruch	Ruth	Baruch
Ezekiel	Baruch	Susanna	Letter of Jeremiah
XII Prophets	Letter of Jeremiah	Esther	Ezekiel
Daniel	Ezekiel	Judith	XII Prophets
Bel	XII Prophets	Ezra	Daniel
Ruth	Susanna	Nehemiah	Bel
Susanna	Daniel		Ruth
Esther	Bel		Susanna
Judith	Psalms		Esther
Bar Sira	Odes		Judith
1-2 Chron.	Esther		Ezra-Neh.
Apoc. of Baruch	Judith		Bar Sira
IV Ezra	Ezra + Nehemiah		1-4 Maccabees
Ezra	Bar Sira		3 Ezra
Nehemiah	1-3 Maccabees		Tobit
1-4 Maccabees			

One thing about these lists which will at once cause surprise is the position of Job immediately after the Pentateuch. This in fact reflects a very old tradition that Job was to be identified with Jobab, mentioned in Genesis 10:29. As a result of this identification, which placed Job in the time of the Patriarchs, the book of Job was placed in chronological sequence, between the Pentateuch and the books of Joshua and Judges. It is very likely that this tradition was also familiar to the community which produced the Dead Sea Scrolls, for it is only the Pentateuch and the book of Job which were ever copied in the Old Hebrew script, rather than in the current Hebrew script (taken over from Aramaic) in which all the other Dead Sea Scrolls are written.

Chronological considerations of this sort explain other striking features in the Milan manuscript: the Psalms, ascribed to David, are consequently placed between Samuel and Kings. This sequence is still preserved in the Cambridge manuscript. In similar fashion, those books traditionally ascribed to Solomon are placed after Kings.

The Milan manuscript alone reflects the ordering of the Hebrew Bible when it separates Chronicles from Kings; in the other three manuscripts Chronicles has been attached to Kings, just as is the case in modern translations of the Old Testament.

One other interesting feature to notice is the sequence of Ruth, Susanna, Esther, and Judith in three of these manuscripts. This group of books was not infrequently copied separately and given the collective title of "The Book of the Women."

In the East Syriac tradition from the ninth century onwards another, larger, grouping of books became common; this was given the title of *Beth Mawthbe*, or "Sessions," and it consists of Joshua, Judges, Samuel, Kings, Proverbs, Qohelet, Ruth, Song of Songs, Bar Sira, and Job. It is unclear what rationale lies behind this combination of books, or why it was given this particular name.

In the New Testament there is much less scope for differing orderings of the books. The Curetonian manuscript of the Old Syriac Gospels is unique in providing the sequence Matthew, Mark, John, Luke. A feature that is regularly found in Peshitta manuscripts, and which goes against the sequence of books familiar today, is the presence of the major Catholic Epistles (James, 1 Peter, 1 John) immediately after Acts and before the Pauline Epistles. The British and Foreign Bible Society's edition (1920) retains the proper Peshitta sequence, but other editions all alter the order and give the standard one instead.

How Is The Biblical Text Divided Up?

Before the advent of printed Syriac Bibles the reader did not have the benefit of having the text divided up into chapters and verses. In fact the chapter divisions familiar today only go back to archbishop Stephen Langton in the early thirteenth century, while the verse divisions are even more recent since they were introduced only in the sixteenth century. This does not mean, however, that numbered divisions were not present at an earlier date in Syriac biblical manuscripts. In contrast to the situation in Greek biblical manuscripts, where many different chapter divisions and numberings are to be found, a remarkably uniform system of numbering is to be found in Syriac manuscripts from the seventh century onwards. These chapter divisions (in Syriac, *shohe*) are usually very different from those in modern printed Bibles. The two earliest examples of this numbering are both East Syriac Gospel manuscripts (of 600 and 615), and this may suggest that the idea originated at the famous School of Nisibis, well known for its biblical studies. Before long, however, it is found in universal use, applied to both the New and the Old Testaments (the earliest manuscripts for the latter using this system are from the eighth century).

In the New Testament each Gospel has its own numbers, while in the case of Acts and the Catholic Epistles on the one hand, and the Pauline Epistles on the other, there is a continuous numbering for each. As can be seen from the Table below, the biblical books are divided up into slightly larger blocks of text than is the case with the chapter divisions of printed Bibles.

TABLE 3:

Numbers of Text Divisions in Syriac New Testament Manuscripts

Matthew	Mark	Luke	John	Acts + Catholic Epistles	Pauline Epistles
22	13	23	20	30	55

The numbers giving this system of text division are still retained in the margins of the British and Foreign Bible Society's standard edition of the Peshitta New Testament.

A later refinement was to provide a second, cumulative, set of numbers covering all the books of the Peshitta New Testament, or groups of books in the Old Testament.

In the case of the Gospels, where there are four different accounts of much the same events, an ingenious system of cross-referencing between the Gospels had been devised in the fourth century by Ammonius of Alexandria. The text of each Gospel is divided up into units which were numbered serially, and under each serial number (or "canon," as it was designated) there is a second number provided, ranging from 1 to 10: this second number indicated which of ten tables (known as "canon tables") one should look up to find a concordance giving the correspondence between the canon numbers in two or more Gospels (each canon table indicated a different combination of Gospels).

A letter, explaining how the system worked, had been written by Eusebius of Caesarea (best known as the first Church historian), addressed to a certain Carpianus, and this was translated into Syriac perhaps in the early fifth century.[5] At the same time the system was introduced into Syriac Gospel manuscripts, but in an improved form. The Syriac adaptor made two important innovations. In the first place, he made it into a more precise tool by diminishing the size of the text units, thus increasing the number of text units, or "canons," in each Gospel (thus Matthew has 355 canons in Greek, but 426 in Syriac). The second innovation consisted in the provision of a miniature concordance at the bottom of each page of the Gospel text. This would indicate the correspondence between the current Gospel canon numbers and their counterparts for any parallel passages in other Gospels. These convenient "foot harmonies," as they are often called, are already present in the very early Peshitta Gospel manuscripts of the sixth century, but they do not appear in any Greek manuscripts until considerably later.

Scribes of Gospel manuscripts with these "Ammonian" numbers would often provide the ten canon tables at the beginning of the manuscript in a decorative form, and many fine examples of this practice can be found in Syriac Gospel manuscripts, one of the earliest being in the illustrated "Rabbula Gospels," dated 586.

What happens in Harklean Gospel manuscripts? Since the aim of the revision was to bring the Syriac text closer to the Greek, the expectation might be that the Harklean would revert to the Greek numbering of the canons; on the other hand, since the Syriac numbering represented a tool that possessed much greater precision, one might alternatively expect that it would be retained. A study of the practice in those Harklean manuscripts which have the canon numbers in fact shows that the dilemma thus posed was not fully resolved, for some Harklean manuscripts retain the more

---

[5] On this see G. H. Gwilliam, "The Ammonian Sections, the Eusebian Canons and harmonizing tables in the Syriac Tetraevangelium," *Studia Biblica et Ecclesiastica* 2 (1890), 241–72.

refined Syriac system, while others (perhaps the majority) reproduce the Greek numbering. Maybe it was Thomas of Harkel himself who accompanied his revision with the Greek numbering, and then at a later date someone who was aware of the superiority of the Syriac system, substituted the Syriac numbering.

Two examples will serve to illustrate how the system works, and to indicate how the Syriac numbering differs from that of the Greek.

The Baptism of Christ is recorded in all four Gospels, Matthew 3:13–17, Mark 1:9–11, Luke 3:21–22, and John 1:32–34. In the Syriac system these passages are broken up into units as follows:

Matthew, four units (numbered 15–18)   Mark, three units (numbered 8–10)

Luke, two units (numbered 15–16)   John, three units(numbered 16–18)

By contrast, the Greek (normally followed in Harklean manuscripts) has only two units for Matthew, and one each for the other three Gospels. The greater number of units in the Syriac system allows for considerably greater precision in the indication of parallels, as the tables below show. In these the serial number of each unit is followed by a slash and then the number of the relevant canon table. In the two examples below, the only tables to feature are tables 1 (for passages in all four Gospels), 4 (for passages only in Matthew and Mark), 5 (for passages only in Matthew and Luke), and 10 (for passages only in one Gospel). In the first example it will be noticed that verse 33 in John does not follow the sequence of the other three Gospels, and it is only in the Syriac system that this feature is made apparent.

TABLE 4A:

Ammonian Sections: Greek and Syriac Systems

GREEK (and normal HARKLEAN) SYSTEM

Matthew (3:13-17)	Mark (1:9-11)	Luke (3:21-22)	John (1:32-34)
verses 13-15 = 13/10	-	-	-
verses 16-17 = 14/1	= 5/1	=13/1	=15/14

SYRIAC SYSTEM

Matthew	Mark	Luke	John
verse 13 = 15/4	verse 9 = 8/4	-	-
verse 14-15 = 16/10	-	-	-
verse 16 = 17/1	verse 10 = 9/1	verse 21, 22a = 15/1	verse 32 = 16/1
(verse 11b = 13/1)	(verse 8 = 7/1)	(verse 16b = 11/1)	verse 33 = 17/1
verse 17 = 18/1	verse 11 = 10/1	verse 22b = 16/1	verse 34 = 18/1

The Lord's Prayer, by contrast, is only given in two Gospels, Matthew and Luke; in this case too, the Syriac system emerges as the one providing the greater precision, since it indicates that Matthew 6:7–8 does not correspond to Luke 11:1, as is implied by the Greek:

TABLE 4B: Ammonian Sections: Greek and Syriac Systems

GREEK (and normal HARKLEAN) SYSTEM

Matt. 6:7–13 = 43/5	Luke 11:1–4 = 123/5

SYRIAC SYSTEM

Matt. 6:7–8 = part of 56/10	Luke 11:1 = part of 148/10
6:9–13 = 57/5	11:2–4 = 149/5

This Syriac system provides the reader with a wonderfully elegant and clear way of seeing which passages in any one Gospel have parallels in other Gospels, and if so, where to find them: the former information is provided by the number of the canon table, and it is there that the canon number(s) in the parallel texts is given, so that the passage(s) can then be quickly located, if so desired.

In the printed editions of the Syriac Gospels the Ammonian numbers and the canon tables are unfortunately not normally given. They can, however, be conveniently found in Pusey and Gwilliam's critical edition of 1901.

Paul of Tella, in his Old Testament translation from Greek known as the Syrohexapla, and Thomas of Harkel in his revision of the New Testament, took over from their Greek sources yet another way of dividing up the biblical text. The name given to these new divisions retained in Syriac the Greek term *kephalaia*, the exact equivalent of English "chapters" (taken from Latin *capita*, "heads, headings"). This way of dividing up the text was taken over by Jacob of Edessa in his revised translation of certain books of the Old Testament, and it has occasionally been introduced into ordinary Peshitta manuscripts. Accompanying the *kephalaia* numbers one may also find chapter titles, and these are sometimes gathered together at the beginning of the manuscript, thus providing a handy table of contents.

As will be seen later, yet another way of dividing up the biblical text was into numbered lections. This meant that in the Gospels there are no less than four different ways of dividing up the text into numbered blocks. Thus for Matthew there are:

TABLE 5:
Differing Divisions of the Gospel Text

426   Ammonian canons (355 in Greek and most Harclean manuscripts)
22   *shahe/shohe* (the basic Peshitta chapter division)
70   *kephalaia* (principally found in Harclean manuscripts)
74   *qeryane/qeryone*, or lections

It is remarkable how little relationship there is between these different systems in their choice of where to make breaks in the text—and the same applies if one compares them to the chapter divisions familiar from printed Bibles.

Some Famous Manuscripts

Obviously among the most famous manuscripts are the early complete Bibles and those with illustrations, such as the Rabbula Gospels of 586. Syriac can claim the earliest dated biblical manuscript in any language: this happens to be the underwriting of a palimpsest, or re-used manuscript on skin where the first text has been washed out, and then a second text written over it. In this case, enough traces of the original text are still visible to enable the contents to be identified (the Book of Isaiah) and the date at the end to be read, namely 771 of the Seleucid era, which corresponds to AD 459/60.[6] This is only shortly before another Syriac dated biblical manuscript, a Pentateuch written in Amid (Diyarbakir) in 463/4 by a certain deacon John.[7] These two manuscripts happen to be the only dated ones to survive from the fifth century, whereas as many as eight are available from the following century, three of them written in Edessa; one of these three happens to be the oldest surviving dated Gospel manuscript in any language, for the colophon states that it was written in October 510, "in the days of the virtuous man of God, bishop Paul, and John his archdeacon."[8]

The place of writing is given in about two-thirds of biblical manuscripts (for those written before 1200, see Table 6, below). Manuscripts of the fifth to eighth centuries are usually written in an elegant Estrangelo hand, and a particularly fine example of calligraphy is provided by a manuscript written in the church of the Holy Apostles, Edessa, in 756;[9] this has the Gospels in the revision by Thomas of Harkel.

---

[6] British Library, Add. 14512 (5ph1 in the Leiden Peshitta).
[7] British Library, Add. 14425 (5b1 in the Leiden Peshitta).
[8] Deir al-Surian, Syr. 8 (Kamil 12).
[9] Florence, Plut. I.40.

TABLE 6:
Places of Writing of Dated Biblical Manuscripts (before 1200)
(Manuscripts of East Syriac or Melkite origin are designated "E" or "M.")

Date	Contents	Place of Writing
464	Pentateuch	Amid
510	Gospels	Edessa
534	New Testament Epistles	Edessa
541	Ezekiel	Edessa
586	"Rabbula" Gospels	Beth Zagba
600	Gospels (E)	Tel Dinawar (Beth Nuhadra)
600	Psalms	(scribe from Monastery of the Orientals, Edessa)
615	Gospels (E)	Nisibis
633	Gospels	Beth Hala, near Damascus
724	1 Kings	Resh'aina
726	Ezekiel	Resh'aina
736	Gospels	Urem Qastra
756	Gospels (Harklean)	Church of the Apostles, Edessa
768	New Testament (E)	Monastery of Sabrisho' (Beth Qoqe)
770	Ezra, Nehemiah	Monastery of Qartmin (i.e., Mor Gabriel)
816	Gospels	Monastery of St. Michael, Egypt
824	Old and New Testament Lectionary	Harran
874	Psalms	Edessa
894	New Testament (E)	Monastery of Joseph, Awana, near Balad
913	Gospels	near Harran
927	Psalms	Deir al-Surian, Egypt
929	Pentateuch (E)	Monastery of Elia, Mosul
936	Gospels (Harklean)	Deir al-Surian, Egypt
981	New Testament (E)	Nisibis
999	Gospels	Monastery of the Forty Martyrs, Melitene
1023	Gospel Lectionary (M)	Monastery of St. Panteleimon (or, of St. Elia), Black Mountain, near Antioch
1041	Gospel Lectionary	Tagrit
1041	Acts and Epistles Lectionary (M)	Monastery of St. Panteleimon, Black Mountain
1045	Gospel Lectionary (M)	Monastery of St. Elia, Black Mountain
1049	New Testament	Deir al-Surian (probably)
1053	Gospels (Harklean)	Melitene

1055	Gospel Lectionary (Harklean)	Melitene
1069	Gospel Lectionary (M)	Monastery of St. Elia, Black Mountain
1074	Gospel Lectionary (E)	Mosul
1089	Gospel Lectionary (Harklean)	Deir al-Surian
1127	Gospel Lectionary (M)	Qara
1138	Gospel Lectionary (Harklean)	Jerusalem
1149	Gospel Lectionary	Jerusalem
1165	Gospels (Harklean)	Monastery of the Cross, Mountain of Edessa
1170	New Testament (Harklean)	Monastery of the Cross, Mountain of Edessa
1174	Old Testament Prophets	Monastery of St. Barbara, Mountain of Edessa
1178	Gospel Lectionary (M)	Qara
1186	Psalms (M)	Saidnaya
1186	Gospel Lectionary (E)	Monastery of Mar Awgen
1188	Gospels	near Balad
1189	Gospel Lectionary (E)	Monastery of St. Michael, Mosul
1190	Gospels	Monastery of the Cross, Tur ʿAbdin
1191	Gospels	Monastery of the Mother of God, Mountain of Edessa
1192	Gospels	Monastery of the Mother of God, Mountain of Edessa
1194	Gospels	Monastery of Mar Jacob the Teacher, Mount Izla
1198	New Testament (E)	Alqosh

The Two Old Syriac Gospel Manuscripts

Two particularly important early, but undated, Gospel manuscripts, both of which are likely to belong to the fifth century, preserve the Old Syriac text. One of these, generally known as the Curetonian, after its first editor, William Cureton, originated from Deir al-Surian in Egypt. It was part of a consignment of old (and often dismembered) manuscript which had been bought by the British Museum in 1842, though it later emerged that three detached leaves from it had gone to Berlin; much more recently, in the 1980s, a single page of the same manuscript was discovered still in the library of the Syrian monastery.[10] The other Old Syriac Gospel manuscript is usually known as Sinaiticus Syriacus, to distinguish it from the famous Greek Sinaiticus, containing the whole Bible. As the name indicates, the manuscript, which is another palimpsest, belongs to the library of the Monastery of St Catherine, on mount Sinai, and is still to be found there— unlike its Greek counterpart, most of which is today in the British Library (though some further folios have recently turned up in the monastery library among the "New Finds," which were discovered after a fire in a blocked-up room). It was Mrs. Agnes Lewis, one of a remarkable pair of Scottish twin sisters, who first realised the potential interest of the manuscript while she and her sister, Mrs. Margaret Gibson, were on a visit to the monastery in 1892, cataloguing the Syriac and Arabic manuscripts. The text written over the Old Syriac Gospels was also an interesting one, for—not inappropriately—it contained a collection of lives of holy women, copied probably in 779.[11] In subsequent years Agnes Lewis was to provide the standard editions of both the lower and the upper texts of this precious manuscript. The Gospel text of the underwriting required much patience in order to read what was still visible, and on a later visit to the monastery to study the manuscript Agnes Lewis noticed that a leaf was missing. Suspecting that some unscrupulous visitor had taken it, she published a notice about it in an academic journal,[12] stating that, if the leaf was returned to her by whoever had taken it, she would place it back in the manuscript. Since this leaf is today in its proper place, her efforts on behalf of the manuscript were evidently successful!

Indication of the importance of these two venerable Old Syriac manuscripts is given by the frequent references to them in modern editions of the Greek Gospels (an example where the reading of Sinaiticus Syriacus has reached a standard modern English translation of the Bible was given above). Though Agnes Lewis and others did heroic work trying to read the underwriting of this manuscript, it should be possible to read much more of it once modern techniques of digital imaging are applied to it.

---

[10] D. McConaughy, "A recently discovered folio of the Old Syriac (Sy c) text of Luke 16:13-17:1," *Biblica* 68 (1987), 85–88.

[11] For the date, see my "Syriac on Sinai: the main connections," in V. Ruggieri and L. Pieralli (eds.), *Eukosmia. Studi miscellanei per il 75 di Vincenzo Poggi S.J.* (Soveria Mannelli, 2003), 106, note 16.

[12] A. S. Lewis, "A leaf stolen from the Sinai Palimpsest," *Expository Times* 13 (1901/2), 405–6.

The First Printed Edition Of The Syriac New Testament (1555)

On learning of the invention of printing in Europe, the Syrian Orthodox
patriarch Ignatius 'Abdallah (1521–1557) sent the priest, Mushe, son of
Ishaq, from the village of Qaluq near Mardin, to Europe to investigate the
possibilities of printing the Syriac New Testament. Mushe, or Moses of
Mardin as he was called in Europe, arrived in Rome sometime before
September 1549, when he copied a collection of Anaphoras there. Although
a few European scholars had already by that time become interested in
Syriac, it took a little while before Mushe was able to get in touch with
them, let alone find someone willing to provide the financial backing
necessary to undertake the printing. By 1553 he was teaching one of the
best European Syriac scholars of the time, Andreas Masius, and about this
time he was put in touch with Johann Albrecht Widmanstetter who himself
was interested in the idea of printing the Syriac New Testament.
Widmanstetter was fortunately able to get the financial patronage of the
Emperor Ferdinand, and so the work could proceed. The handsome
finished product was published in Vienna in 1555, using an elegant
Estrangelo typeface that had specially been designed for the volume. At the
end of each of the Gospels, of Acts, and of the Epistles, Mushe provided a
different Syriac colophon, and with the help of these and the accompanying
Latin ones we can follow the progress of the work: Matthew was printed on
14 February, Mark on 21 March, Luke on 25 April, John on 18 May, the
Epistles in the middle of July, and Acts on 14 August. The generosity of the
emperor Ferdinand is mentioned right at the beginning of the work; there
he is given the title "Emperor of Rome, Germany, Hungary and Bohemia,
and heir of Spain," and reference is also made to his sons, Maximilian,
Ferdinand, and Charles, and daughters (who are left unnamed). By contrast,
it is only at the end of John that Mushe first makes mention of himself and
Widmanstetter:

> The holy Gospel of the four Evangelists, Matthew, Mark, Luke, and
> John, was printed in Syriac characters and in the Syriac language with
> accurate endeavour, being corrected from two other old Syriac copies,
> through the agency of the priest Mushe, son of the priest Ishaq, from
> Beth Nahrin (Mesopotamia), from the region of Sawro (Savur), adjacent
> to the town of Mardin, the disciple and emissary of Mor Ignatius,
> Patriarch of Antioch, to the blessed Fathers, Mor Paulos III and Mor
> Julios III, Popes of Rome; and with the assistance and thoughtful care
> of the blessed believer Yuhanon Albertus Widmanstadius, skilled in
> knowledge, endowed with intelligence, lover of learning, teacher of
> Roman law, counsellor to the Emperor … who has a special love for

the Syrians since he knows the Syriac language and many other languages, who persuaded and got permission from the Emperor to print these books.

It is interesting to see that in the colophon to the Epistles, composed some months later, the wording of Mushe's colophon has changed: Widmanstetter is mentioned first, and it is through his agency that the work is said to have been done. Only right at the end of the colophon does Mushe make mention of himself:

> Pray, brethren, for me, the feeble Mushe, a priest, son of the priest Ishaq, from the region of Sawro near the town of Mardin, because I laboured greatly over these books.

What is the reason for this altered wording? One can readily suppose that, once the Gospels were printed, Widmanstetter read Mushe's colophon to John and objected that Mushe had presented him as playing only a minor role. Accordingly, Mushe worded the later colophon in a way that would be acceptable to Widmanstetter, while nevertheless hinting, by the words "I laboured greatly," that it was in fact him who had done the bulk of the work. This would in fact be only what one would have expected, since it is most unlikely that Widmanstetter would have had a sufficient knowledge of Syriac to do the work on his own.

In the course of the various colophons Mushe makes mention of his own parents (Ishaq and Heleni) and three brothers, the priest Barsaumo, Shem'un and Yeshu', as well as of Widmanstetter's wife, Anna, and his three daughters, Maria, Virginia, and Justinia.

European Syriac scholarship owes a second debt to Mushe, seeing that he was the person who taught Andreas Masius, the man who preserved numerous readings from the now lost manuscript of the Syrohexapla of Joshua.

Subsequent Early Editions Of The Syriac Bible

The second half of the sixteenth century saw the publication of several other editions of the Syriac New Testament, though only one of these was in Syriac characters, the others making use of Hebrew ones. The reason for this was twofold: the scarcity of Syriac type, and the much greater familiarity of European scholars of the time with the Hebrew script. Thus, even in the New Testament volume of the Antwerp Polyglot (vol. 5, 1571), where Syriac script is used, the text was also given a second time, but in Hebrew characters.

These sixteenth-century editions of the Peshitta New Testament do not contain the non-Peshitta books (2 Peter, 2–3 John, Jude, and Revelation). The Syriac text of these only became available in the seventeenth century, when the Harklean Apocalypse was published by Louis de Dieu (Leiden, 1627), and the sixth-century translation of the minor Catholic Epistles by William Pococke (Oxford, 1630). The text of these was added to almost all subsequent European editions, from the Paris polyglot Bible onwards, continuing until the early twentieth century, when the Harklean Apocalypse was replaced by the sixth-century version discovered by John Gwynn (published in 1897).

The first book of the Syriac Old Testament to get into printed form was, not surprisingly, the Psalter. The Maronite printing press at Quzhaya had published an edition in 1610, with both Syriac and Garshuni.[13] The latter preceded the first European editions by fifteen years. In fact, 1625 saw the publication of two separate editions, one by the Maronite scholar Gabriel Sionita (Paris) and the other by Thomas Erpenius (Leiden). The complete Syriac Old Testament came twenty years later, in the last volumes (6–9) of the great Paris Polyglot edition (1629–45; the Syriac New Testament features in volume 5). Closely based, as far as the Syriac is concerned, on the Paris Polyglot was its London counterpart, edited by Brian Walton (1655–67).

The seventeenth, eighteenth, and nineteenth centuries witnessed a surprisingly large number of further editions of parts of the Peshitta Bible, chiefly the New Testament, as can be seen from Table 7, below. The most important of these were some of the nineteenth-century ones.

TABLE 7:
Main Printed Editions of the Peshitta

Whole Bible	Old Testament	Psalms	New Testament	Gospels
			1555 Vienna	
			1569 Geneva	
			1571 Antwerp	
			1574-5 Antwerp	
			1584 Paris	
			1599 Nurenberg	
		1610 Quzhaya		
			1621 Kothen	

---

[13] The alleged edition of 1585 appears never to have existed: see J. Nasrallah, *L'Imprimerie au Liban* (Harisa, 1948), 1–7.

		1625 Paris		
		1625 Leiden		
1645 Paris				
1655-7 London				
			1663 Hamburg	
			1684 Sulzbach	
			1703 Rome	
			1709 Leiden	
			1713 Leipzig	
			1805 Oxford	
			1816 London	
	1823 London		1824 Paris	
			1826 London	
				1828 London
				1829 London
		1846 Istanbul[14]	1846 Urmi	
	1852 Urmi			
		1866 Mosul		
		1874 New York		
	1876-83 Milan	1877 Mosul	1877 Urmi	
		1886 New York		
1887-91 Mosul				
		1891 Urmi		
				1901 Oxford
		1904 Cambridge		
			1905-20 London	
	1913 New York			
		1914 London		
1952 Beirut				
	1966 Leiden			
1979 (UBS)				
			1983 New Knoxville	
			1986 Munster	
1988 (UBS)				

[14] For this, see D. M. Dunlop, "A little known Oriental printing press," *Bulletin of the John Rylands Library Manchester* 38 (1956), 279–81. A Garshuni narrative about the setting up of this press in 1845, by Metropolitan Ya'qub of Jerusalem, is to be found in Mingana Syr. 202 (of 1845).

				1996 Leiden
				1998 Istanbul

Nineteenth- And Twentieth-Century Editions

Earlier printed editions of the Syriac Bible were based on medieval or post-medieval manuscripts. With the exception of Widmanstetter's collaboration with the Syrian Orthodox Mushe of Mardin, European scholars had mainly been in contact with Maronites, and at the end of the sixteenth century the Maronite College had been established in Rome. This was to produce a long line of very distinguished Maronite scholars, one of whom was Gabriel Sionita, the man chiefly responsible for the Syriac text in the Paris Polyglot Bible. As a result of these circumstances, not only were the manuscripts used for editions in many cases fairly recent, but they all belonged to the West Syriac tradition.

In the case of one important early nineteenth-century edition, that of Samuel Lee, a little attention was paid to the need to make use of earlier manuscripts. Although he used as the basis for his edition the text to be found in Walton's Polyglot, he did consult a number of older manuscripts, and among these was the famous "Buchanan codex" of the twelfth century.[15] This illustrated manuscript of the Old Testament had been brought back from India by Claudius Buchanan in 1808, and is today in the Cambridge University Library. The manuscript must have been brought to India a century or so earlier by a Syrian Orthodox bishop, for it was certainly originally copied in the Middle East.

It was only in the nineteenth century, with the Urmi and Mosul editions, that the witness of the East Syriac manuscript tradition first came to be used, though in the case of the Urmi edition it now appears that the text was in fact largely derived from Samuel Lee's edition, which itself for the most part went back to Walton's Polyglot.

A much more important development of the nineteenth century, however, was the acquisition by the British Museum, London, of many very old manuscripts from Deir al-Surian, many of which were biblical. Only then did it become possible to base an edition on very early sources. For the Old Testament a magnificent start was made with the photolithographic reprint of the sixth- or seventh-century manuscript in the Ambrosian Library, Milan, published by A. M. Ceriani (1876–83). Early Gospel manuscripts originating from Deir al-Surian are particularly plentiful, and an excellent critical edition, based on these, was produced by P. Pusey and

---

[15] Cambridge Oo.1.1 (12a1 in the Leiden Peshitta).

J. Gwynn in 1901, accompanied by a facing Latin translation. Another academic edition which used all the early manuscripts available was that produced for the Psalms by W. E. Barnes (1904). Use was made of these two works, and of unpublished collations of early manuscripts, in the British and Foreign Bible Society's editions of the New Testament (1905–20), Psalms (1914), and Pentateuch (1914, in Estrangelo script). The first two of these, in the western Syriac script, have been frequently reprinted.

After a gap of nearly half a century scholarly work on the Syriac Bible resumed in a big way with a major project to produce a critical edition of the Peshitta Old Testament. The idea was first launched at an international congress of Old Testament scholars in 1953, and in 1959 the project was entrusted to the University of Leiden, where the Peshitta Institute was set up. With remarkable speed a preliminary (but nonetheless very full and detailed) list of manuscripts was produced (1961), and in due course a specimen volume appeared (1966). This has been followed by editions of individual books or groups of books, filling 13 volumes so far. The text printed in these volumes is that of the manuscript in the Ambrosian Library, Milan, with a few modifications. This provides the reader with a considerably earlier stage in the textual history of the Peshitta Old Testament than is available in the other printed Syriac Bibles.

Another major academic project on the Syriac Bible, based in Münster, concerns the New Testament. Here the aim is to provide the text of both the Peshitta and the Harklean, both based on the earliest and best manuscripts available, and to illustrate this with a collection of quotations taken from early Syriac writers. For practical reasons, the first volume to appear (in 1986) covered those of the Catholic Epistles which form part of the Peshitta canon (i.e., James, 1 Peter, 1 John), and the three further volumes that have so far been published cover all the Letters of St. Paul.

A further handy edition of the Syriac New Testament which is based on early manuscripts was produced in 1983 by The Way International, using the Estrangelo script. For the books which are not part of the Peshitta canon, use has been made of the sixth-century versions (and not—despite the Preface's statement!—the Harklean).

For practical purposes, several of the nineteenth-century editions of the Syriac Bible have been re-issued in more recent editions. The edition of the Old Testament, published by the American Mission in Urmi in 1852, was reprinted by the Trinitarian Bible Society in New York in 1913, incorporating some minor alterations made by Yausep d-Kelaita, a notable scholar of the Church of the East. The great Mosul edition of the Peshitta Bible (1887–91), edited by the Syrian Catholic metropolitan of Damascus,

Mor Clemens Joseph David, and with a preface by the Chaldean metropolitan of Amid (Diyarbakir), Jirjis ʿAbdishoʿ Khayyat, was reprinted, again with some slight modifications, in Beirut in 1952. Both the Urmi and the Mosul editions are in the East Syriac script, and so of little practical use for the Syrian Orthodox or Maronites. Designed for their needs (and with a commendation by the Syrian Orthodox Patriarch Mor Ignatius Yaʿqub III) is the United Bible Societies' edition. When first issued, in 1979, both the Old and the New Testament reproduced the text edited by Samuel Lee (New Testament, 1816; Old Testament 1823), but in reprints since 1988 the text of the New Testament was changed, and instead of Lee's edition, that of the British and Foreign Bible Society's edition (1920) has been employed. In practical terms this means that the New Testament text is now based on the earliest available manuscripts, and for the non-Peshitta books, Revelation is in the sixth-century translation, rather than in the Harklean version.

The British and Foreign Bible Society's edition of the Syriac Gospels has also been used in the very helpful Comparative Edition of the Syriac Gospels, edited by George Kiraz (1996), where the Peshitta (here in vocalized Estrangelo script) is aligned with both the earlier Old Syriac, and with the later Harklean. Another recent edition of the Gospels, also produced by Syrian Orthodox scholars, is that published in Istanbul by the Monastery of Mor Gabriel in Tur ʿAbdin (1994). This is intended for practical Bible Study, and (for the first time in any edition of the Syriac Bible) is provided with ample cross references and other useful aids.

The Main Editions Of Other Syriac Translations

The early seventh-century translation of the Greek Septuagint, known today as the Syrohexapla but traditionally referred to as "the Seventy," was so massive that it was very rarely copied as a whole, and even then, this was in two volumes. One such volume, dating from the eighth or ninth century and containing the second half of the Old Testament, survives today in Milan, and a beautiful lithographic edition of this was published by A. M. Ceriani in 1874. The first volume must have been in Europe in the sixteenth century, for the Andreas Masius, the pupil of Mushe of Mardin, published a few readings from it. What became of this manuscript is completely unknown: it will have been far too big just to get mislaid! To make up for this lamentable loss, the great German scholar Paul de Lagarde collected together what could be recovered of the text from manuscripts that contained only parts of the text, and subsequently his collection (1892) has been supplemented by various scholars. Of particular interest are two photographic editions, published by the great Estonian Syriac scholar, Arthur Vööbus (1909–1988); one of these is of an eighth-century manuscript of Isaiah preserved in the library of the Syrian Orthodox Monastery of St. Mark in Jerusalem, while the other is of a twelfth-century manuscript of the Pentateuch formerly in Midyat. Although this manuscript is later in date it is of especial importance in that it contains many passages for which the Syrohexapla text had hitherto been completely lost. It has already been noted that the Harklean had first made its appearance in print in 1627 in L. de Dieu's edition of the Revelation of John. Unfortunately the handsome Serto type of this edition does not match up to the quality of its text (which was to get reprinted many times): de Dieu had derived it from a late manuscript whose text had become somewhat corrupted in the course of its previous transmission. It is intriguing to note that this manuscript had been copied by "Caspar from the land of the Hindus"; this Caspar is known to have been in Rome in 1580 when he copied another manuscript there. It was not until three and a half centuries later, in 1978, that a much better Harklean text of the Revelation of John, to be found in a thirteenth-century manuscript in Mardin, was eventually published (by Arthur Vööbus) in a photographic edition.

The rest of the Harklean New Testament had to wait until the end of the eighteenth century, when Joseph White published it over a number of years (1778–1803). In his view, the text represented the work of Philoxenus, and not that of Thomas of Harkel, and so he gave it the misleading title "Versio Philoxeniana."This gave rise to over 150 years of argument among scholars over whether or not he was correct, and it is only fairly recently that the matter has now been finally resolved, and it is now certain that the text he published was the Harklean, and not the Philoxenian. The need for a new edition of the Harklean has long been felt, and in recent years the Research Institute for New Testament Text in Münster has initiated the important new edition which has already been mentioned above, since it aligns the Harklean text with that of the Peshitta. The oldest and most important manuscript for the Letters of St. Paul happens to be another manuscript in the library of the Monastery of St. Mark in Jerusalem.

The Harklean Gospels feature in another aligned edition, that of George Kiraz, also mentioned above. For this, use has been made of a manuscript in the Vatican Library in Rome which is several centuries older than the manuscript used by Joseph White.

Until recently only extracts of Jacob of Edessa's further revision of certain Old Testament books had been published, but now a complete edition of his revision of I–II Samuel has been published by Alison

Salvesen,[16] using a typeface which is modelled on the beautiful Estrangelo handwriting of the single surviving manuscript, copied in 719, only eleven years after Jacob's death.

Lectionaries

Before the wide availability of printed Syriac Bibles most people would encounter the Bible through hearing it, rather than reading it, and this would take place in the course of the various liturgical services for which biblical readings, or lections, were specified. The choice of lections varied considerably from one locality to another, and there was also a difference between monastic and non-monastic usage. In the Church of the East both the monastic and the non-monastic (or Cathedral) lectionary cycles had become fixed by about the ninth century, which is about the time of the earliest extant manuscripts. The monastic lectionary was based on the usage of the Upper Monastery in Mosul, while the non-monastic cycle derived from the practice in the Cathedral church of the Catholicos, originally in Seleucia-Ctesiphon (the Sasanian winter capital). Eventually, however, in the Church of the East the monastic usage supplanted the cathedral cycle altogether.

In the Syrian Orthodox Church there has always been much greater flexibility and local variation and it is only in modern times, with printed lectionary texts, that usage is becoming standardized. In the early Middle Ages, for example, no two lectionary manuscripts will provide exactly the same choice of lections, although there is often a certain amount of overlap (the choice of biblical passages for certain feasts, of course, will be limited). Sometimes, however, a Syrian Orthodox lectionary manuscript will provide a very individual choice of lections: this is the case with a lectionary compiled by the Patriarch Athanasius V and preserved in a manuscript of AD 1000;[17] this gives lections from both the Old Testament and the New Testament Epistles (no doubt there was once a separate manuscript containing Athanasius' selection of Gospel lections).

In recent years two printed Syrian Orthodox New Testament lectionaries have been published, both by Metropolitan Julius Cicek, at the monastery of St. Ephrem in Holland; one covers the Gospels (1987) and the other the Epistles (1992). In these, the allocation of biblical passages to

---

[16] A. Salvesen, *The Books of Samuel in the Syriac Version of Jacob of Edessa* (Monographs of the Peshitta Institute 10; Leiden, 1999); an English translation is also provided.
[17] British Library, Add. 17139 (Wright, *Catalogue*, no CCXXIV).

the cycle of the liturgical year in general follows the list of lections published by the late Metropolitan Yuhanon Dolabani of Mardin in 1955.[18]

How Does The Reader Find The Place?

A biblical book is only rarely read in sequence in the course of the liturgical year, and even if it is, there will be many interruptions when a more appropriate passage is required for a particular feast or commemoration. This of course means that the person reading the lection could easily have difficulty in finding the place. A number of different solutions to this problem were found of the course of time.

In the small number of fifth-century biblical manuscripts that survive there seem to be no special indications pointing to liturgical reading. This, however, changes in the sixth century, for now the scribes of biblical manuscripts sometimes introduce into the text a rubric stating that this was where the lection for a particular feast or occasion began.

A single example of a list of biblical readings throughout the liturgical year is preserved from the sixth century.[19] For the Gospels the lections are identified by means of the number in the Eusebian canon tables, while for other books there is just the name of the book, followed by the opening and closing words of the lection. The list is remarkable both for the large number of lections for any one commemoration, and for the length of the lections.

In sixth-century biblical manuscripts the indications for lections are rather haphazard and certainly do not even meet all the most important the requirements of the liturgical year. A remedy to this unsatisfactory situation is first to be found in manuscripts of the seventh and eighth centuries, where a table of lections may be given at the beginning of a biblical manuscript. These lections will be arranged in accordance with the needs of the liturgical year, and not in the biblical sequence of occurrence. In order to locate the lection in the text, however, a set of cross references is provided: in the lection table the relevant quire and page number is given, while in the biblical text a marginal letter *q* (for *qeryono*, "lection") is given at

---

[18] An English version of this list has been published by Mor Cyril Afrem Karim, *Scripture Readings for Sundays and Feast Days according to the Tradition of the Syrian Orthodox Church of Antioch* (Teaneck, NJ, 2000).

[19] In British Library, Add. 14528; the text was edited and commented on by F. C. Burkitt, "The early Syriac Lectionary system," *Proceedings of the British Academy* 1921/3, 301–28. Another (damaged) folio belonging to this manuscript still remains at Deir al-Surian. (I am most grateful to Bishop Mattaos and Fr. Bigoul, of the Monastery, for permission to refer to this).

the beginning, and *sh* (for *shlem*, "it is ended") at the conclusion of each lection.

This practice was sometimes applied to older manuscripts, where one can readily see that the lectionary indications have been added by a later hand. Indeed, there are a few cases where a sixth-century manuscript has evidently still been in use over half a millennium later, as is indicated by the presence of lectionary markings in a twelfth- or thirteenth-century hand.

The idea of extracting the lections from the biblical text and then arranging them in the sequence of the liturgical year seems to have been an innovation of the eighth or ninth century in the Syriac Churches. The earliest surviving true lectionary manuscripts of this sort in Syriac date from the ninth century. For this purpose, readings from different parts of the Bible were collected into separate books. The Old Testament lections were sometimes provided on their own, or they might be combined in the same manuscript with those from the Acts and the Epistles. The Gospel lections are normally on their own, and in the twelfth and thirteenth centuries these Gospel lectionaries are often masterpieces of Syriac calligraphy; many were also accompanied by illustrations.[20]

In the Church of the East a remarkably stable lectionary system developed, one for use in ordinary churches, the other for monasteries; in the course of time, however, the monastic system, associated with the "Upper Monastery" in Mosul, became the standard one everywhere.[21] Evidence for the use of the East Syriac lectionary as far east as Dunhuang in China has recently turned up, when a fragment with lections for Holy Week taken from Galatians and 1 Corinthians was identified.[22]

Among the Syrian Orthodox, the person who was initially responsible for putting the lections together had to make a further choice of which biblical text to use. Normally, of course, it was the Peshitta that he chose, but on occasion use might be made of the Syrohexapla in the Old Testament and of the Harklean in the New Testament (where in practice

---

[20] For these, see *The Hidden Pearl*, II, Chapter 7, together with the Annotation in *Hugoye* 5:1 (2002), 96–7.

[21] For the East Syriac Lectionary systems, see W. Macomber, "The Chaldean Lectionary system of the Cathedral Church of Kokhe," *Orientalia Christiana Periodica* 33 (1967), 483–516; P. Kannookadan, *The East Syrian Lectionary* (Mar Thoma Yogam Publications 4; Rome, 1991); K. D. Jenner, "The development of the Syriac Lectionary systems," *The Harp* 10 (1997), 9–24.

[22] See W. Klein and J. Tubach, "Ein syrisch-christliches Fragment aus Dunhang, China," *Zeitschrift der deutschen morgenländischen Gesellschaft* 144 (1994), 1–13, together with the further note, by H. Kaufhold, in 145 (1995), 49–60.

this was limited to the Gospels). In a few cases a Gospel Lectionary might exclusively employ the text of the Harklean.

A further development in the case of Gospel Lectionaries was the creation of a harmony of all four evangelists for the readings to be used during Holy Week. The arrangement of this harmony has no connection with that found in Tatian's Diatessaron, and indeed two different arrangements are found in Gospel Lectionaries, one of which is associated with a certain Rabban Daniel and his disciple Isaac.

In some Gospel lectionaries of the twelfth and thirteenth centuries the lections are numbered, even though the numbers do not have any particular function; thus in a deluxe copy which the scribe, Bakos (from Beth Khudeida, but working in Edessa) himself donated to Deir al-Surian in 1230,[23] there are 331 lections in all. Probably this use of numbers reflects a further development that had taken place at an uncertain date, but certainly by the twelfth century. Instead of making use of separate lectionaries with the contents arranged according to the liturgical year, this new system reverted to having straightforward biblical manuscripts, but with lectionary headings incorporated into the biblical text (in this respect, a reversion to much earlier usage), but with each lection numbered in its biblical sequence (thus, for example, Matthew is divided up into lections numbered 1–74). The key to which reading to use at which time is now provided in tables arranged according to the liturgical year, accompanied by the appropriate number of the lection. These tables are located either at the beginning or end of the manuscript. The reference system is quick and easy to use.

Elements of this last system can be found reproduced in certain printed edition, in particular in Samuel Lee's edition of the New Testament (reproduced in the original printing, 1979, of the United Bible Societies' edition of the Syriac Bible).

In the two Syrian Orthodox printed lectionaries, mentioned above, a combination of two systems is found. In both the lections are arranged according to the liturgical year (the practice of all lectionaries proper), and in the Pauline Lectionary they are also accompanied by numbers (as in Bakos's Lectionary of 1230). The Gospel Lectionary has a separate table of lections in the sequence of the liturgical year, giving page numbers (which are of course in sequence), while the Pauline Lection in an index at the end has the references, in biblical sequence, to all the passages used, indexing them by means of their lection number. This sort of biblical index is in fact a modern refinement that Bakos would not have considered necessary.

---

[23] British Library, Or. 8729.

The Psalter

The book of the Psalms has played a central role in the liturgical and monastic life of all the Churches. A number of different features are distinctive of the Syriac Psalter and the way in which it is used.

Anyone who looks up references to the Psalms in early Christian writers will quickly become aware of the practical problems of numbering the Psalms. Although the Syriac and Greek translations of the Hebrew book of Psalms all end up with Psalm 150, from Psalm 9 to Psalm 147 there are numerous differences in numbering between the three languages, as a result of which great frustration can be caused if a reference is given without it being clear which numbering is being quoted. These differences can most readily be seen in tabular form:

TABLE 8:
Numberings of the Psalms in Hebrew, Syriac and Greek

Hebrew		Peshitta		Septuagint
1-8	=	1-8	=	1-8
9-10	=	9-10		9:1-21 + 9:22-39
11-113	=	11-113		10-112
114-115		114		113:1-8 + 9-26
116:1-9		115:1-9		114
116:10-19		115:10-19		115
117-146		116-145	=	116-145
147:1-11		146	=	146
147:12-20		147	=	147
148-150	=	148-150	=	148-150

English translations will follow the Hebrew numbering (unless, of course, they are specifically translated from the Septuagint or Peshitta). Another source of confusion is that the verse numbering within a psalm may be slightly different, depending whether or not the psalm title has been included in the numbering.

The Hebrew Psalms all have titles, which give the attribution (usually to David), sometimes accompanied by certain rubrics whose meaning is often very obscure. These titles also feature in the Greek Septuagint, though not always in the same form. By contrast, the original Syriac translation of the Psalms simply omitted the Psalm titles, as being too obscure, and in any case the rubrics, where given, were no longer operative. This left a vacuum which in due course came to be filled and quite different sets of titles were introduced. Since the East and West Syriac traditions have different titles, these cannot have been introduced in either tradition before about the second half of the fifth century or later.[24] For the most part both the East and West Syriac titles aim to provide a historical setting for each particular psalm. In the Ambrosian Library's manuscript of the Peshitta almost all the Psalms are attributed to David and are said to refer to episodes in his lifetime (this explains the position of the Psalter between Samuel and Kings in this manuscript, noted above). Later West Syriac manuscripts may have some additional (or alternative) information, of a specifically Christian character; this later stage is reflected in the Psalm titles given in S. Lee's edition, now reprinted by the United Bible Society. In the East Syriac tradition, although David is normally the presumed author, the titles quite often state that he his speaking about some future time; this is most frequently the time of either Hezekiah or the Exile and Return, but in seventeen cases the time specified is that of the Maccabees. Only in four instances is the prophecy said to refer to Christ (Psalms 2, 8, 45, and 110). Three examples will illustrate the differences between the titles:

[24] The East Syriac Psalm titles were edited (without translation) by W. Bloemendaal, *The Headings of the Psalms in the East Syrian Church* (Leiden, 1960). An edition of the West Syriac, by D. G. K. Taylor, is in preparation.

Psalm 8
("O Lord, our Lord, how majestic is your name in all the earth…")

Hebrew: To the choirmaster: according to the Gittith. A Psalm of David.

Ambrosian manuscript: Uttered by David when the people and the priest carried the Ark of Adonay to convey it to the house that David had build for it.

Lee and UBS edition: A prophecy that sucklings, babes and children would praise the Lord with Hosannas.

East Syriac tradition: He prophesies concerning Christ our Lord, and also indicates to us concerning the distinction between (his) natures.

Psalm 22
("My God, my God, why have you forsaken me…")

Hebrew: To the choirmaster: according to The Hind of the Dawn. A Psalm of David.

Ambrosian manuscript: Uttered by David when his persecutors were going around jeering at him.

Lee and UBS edition: By David, when his persecutors were mocking him, and about the passion of Christ and the call of the Gentiles.

East Syriac tradition: Uttered by David by way of prayer when he was chased by Absalom.

Psalm 44
("We have heard with our ears, O God, …")

Hebrew: To the choirmaster: A Maskil of the Sons of Korah.

Ambrosian manuscript: Uttered by David concerning the people who perished at Horeb.

Lee and UBS edition: By the sons of Qorah, as the people were singing in Horeb with Moses. Again, a supplication of the prophets, of David and the rest. And for us, success and victory over adversaries.

East Syriac tradition: The supplication of the Maccabees when they were under constraint from Antiochus to sacrifice to idols.

It is interesting that many of the Psalm titles in the Ambrosian manuscript are also to be found in the mid sixth-century commentary on the Psalms by Daniel of Salah, while the East Syriac ones are derived from the commentary by the Greek biblical scholar Theodore of Mopsuestia.

The Psalms have always played a very important role in liturgical, and in particular in monastic, tradition. For convenience in the recitation of the Psalter a number of different ways of dividing up the Psalter came into being. Here again the East and West Syriac traditions went their separate ways, even though one of the terms used for a group of psalms was shared.

According to the Syrian Orthodox division, the Psalter is divided up into fifteen *marmyotho*, and within each *marmitho* there are four *shubohe*, making sixty in all. By contrast, in the East Syriac tradition there are 20 larger groups, called *hullale*, and within each of these there are two or three *marmyatha*, making fifty-seven in all. The origins of some of these terms are obscure, but *marmitho* may originally have referred to an "interposed" prayer, said at the beginning of each *marmitho*. In both West and East Syriac tradition a refrain was also added; those for the East Syriac Psalter (known as *qanone*) are attributed to Mar Aba in the mid-fifth century, and already appear in a very early fragment of the Middle Persian translation of the Psalter.

Melkite manuscripts of the Psalms have yet another way of dividing up the psalms into groups, corresponding to the standard Greek Orthodox system, with twenty *kathismata*, each consisting of three *shubohe*, making sixty *shubohe* in all.

Syriac Psalters, like Greek ones, also have a series of Odes (in Syriac, *teshbhotho*), consisting of psalm-like poetic passages from elsewhere in the Old or New Testament. Here again there is a difference in usage between the East and West Syriac tradition. In the former there are normally three Odes, consisting of Exodus 15:1–21, Isaiah 42:10–13 + 45:8, and Deuteronomy 32:1–43; to these three a fourth, Daniel 3:57–88, is often added, and it is this group of four Odes that is also found in the Maronite tradition. In the Syrian Orthodox there is (as is often the case) some flexibility; normally there are six Odes, with two or three New Testament ones (Luke 1:46–55, Mary; Luke 1:68–79, Zechariah; Matthew 5:3–12, Beatitudes) added to the first three Odes already mentioned. A smaller number of Syrian Orthodox psalm manuscripts agree with the Melkite psalters which have nine Old Testament Odes, the additional ones being 1 Samuel 2:1–10; Habbakuk 3:2–19; Isaiah 26:9–20; Jonah 2:3–10; Daniel 3:26–56, and 3:57–88.

These Odes are not printed after the Psalms in any of the western printed editions of the Syriac Bible. In the Syrian Catholic edition prepared by Joseph David, and printed in Mosul in 1877, however, ten Odes are provided, in the order: Deuteronomy 32, Exodus 15, I Samuel 2, Habbakuk 3, Isaiah 26, Jonah 2, Daniel 3 (both passages), Isaiah 42 + 45, and Isaiah 38. The presence of the last Ode (the Prayer of Hezekiah) is remarkable, for it is only very rarely found in manuscripts of the Psalter, and is first attested there in the ninth-century complete Old Testament in Florence. An East Syriac Psalter printed in the Middle East and containing the Odes, is the Urmi edition of 1891, published by the Archbishop of Canterbury's educational mission to the Church of the East in Urmi. This contains the normal three Odes of the East Syriac tradition, but with Deuteronomy 32 divided into two separate Odes.

The Fate Of An Additional Psalm

Syriac and Greek Psalm manuscripts normally have an extra Psalm, Psalm 151, and the underlying Hebrew text of this Psalm has only recently turned up among the Dead Sea Scrolls. It features there in a rather well preserved manuscript from Qumran, Cave 11, along with some other non-biblical psalms. Psalm 151 only rarely appears in printed editions of the Psalter. In the original forms of Samuel Lee's editions of the Old Testament (1823) and the Psalms (1825), Psalm 151 indeed appeared, having been taken over from Walton's Polyglot. Objections, however, were raised by the General Committee of the British and Foreign Bible Society (who had sponsored the edition), on the grounds that "apocryphal" material, not to be found in the Hebrew Bible, should not be included. Accordingly, Psalm 151 was excised from as many copies as possible of these two editions, and from all further printings of them.[25] As a result, Psalm 151 is today only to be found in the rather rare (it seems) copies of the original editions that have escaped this treatment. Ironically, now that the Hebrew text of Psalm 151 has actually turned up, Psalm 151 is still absent from the United Bible Societies' re-edition of Lee's text, since a copy of his edition has been used where the offending text had been excised!

---

[25] On this, see P. Dirksen, "Lee's edition of the Syriac Old Testament and the Psalms," in A. S. van der Woude (ed.), *In Quest of the Past. Studies on Israelite Religion, Literature and Prophetism* (Oudtestamentische Studien 26; 1990), 63–71.

Yet Further Psalms

One twelfth-century East Syriac Psalter and a few other non-biblical manuscripts contain four further Psalms, 152–5, and for two of these (154 and 155) the underlying Hebrew original is now recovered, in the same manuscript from Cave 11. By remarkable good fortune we know a little about how these apocryphal Hebrew Psalms reached Syriac about AD 800. In one of his Letters (no. 47)[26] the East Syriac Patriarch Timothy I tells of a discovery of some "Dead Sea Scrolls" that took place about 1150 years before the famous discoveries of the present century. Curiously enough, the circumstances of their finding were identical in both cases. This is how Timothy relates the exciting story:

> We have heard from certain Jews who are worthy of credence, who have recently been converted to Christianity, that some ten years ago some books were discovered in the vicinity of Jericho, in a cave-dwelling in the mountain. They say that the dog of an Arab who was hunting game went into a cleft after an animal and did not come out again. His owner then went in after him and found a chamber inside the mountain containing many books. The huntsman went to Jerusalem and reported this to some Jews. A lot of people set off and arrived there; they found books of the Old Testament, and apart from that, other books in Hebrew script. Because the person who told me knows the script and is skilled in reading it, I asked him about certain verses adduced in our New Testament as being from the Old Testament, but of which there is no mention at all in the Old Testament, neither among us Christians, nor among the Jews. He told me that they were to be found in the books that had been discovered there.

After mentioning a number of such passages, Timothy continues:

> Now that Hebrew man told me, "We found a David (that is, a Psalter) among those books, containing more than two hundred psalms."

A Revised Peshitta Psalter

Mention has already been made, in connection with the Odes, of the Mosul edition (1877) of the Psalter. This was the product of a remarkable work of scholarship: as the preface (by the Syrian Catholic bishop Cyrillus Behnam Benni) explains, the Peshitta text had been compared with the Hebrew, and as a result "corruptions (*mendis*)" in the Syriac had been removed and the

---

[26] There is an English translation in my *A Brief Outline of Syriac Literature* (SEERI, Moran Etho Series 9; Kottayam, 1997), 245–50.

text corrected in accordance with the original Hebrew text.[27] If one compares the text of this edition with that of the Peshitta, one will indeed find a certain number of places, both in the Psalms and in the Odes, where the text has carefully been brought closer into line with the Hebrew. Thus, for example, in the much used Psalm 51, "Have mercy on me, O God, in Your compassion…," just over a dozen alterations of this sort have been made. Several of these occur together, in verse 8, where the two texts read:

Peshitta	Mosul Psalter (1877)
Fill me with your delight and joy, and let my humble bones rejoice.	Cause me to hear delight and your joy, and let the bones you have shattered rejoice.

In the case of each alteration, the Mosul edition represents the Hebrew text more exactly. (In passing, it is worth noting that the English Revised Standard Version happens to prefer the Peshitta's reading "Fill me" at the beginning of the verse). It is clear that Joseph David, who must have had a good knowledge of Hebrew, carried out his revision with great care. As part of his task he has also provided for the first time a Syriac translation of the psalm headings as they appear in the Hebrew text.

Polyglot Bibles

One usually associates the idea of having a truly polyglot Bible with sixteenth-century European scholarship, but in fact an unknown Syrian Orthodox scholar, probably working in Egypt, produced such a work at least a century before the first European polyglot biblical text (this had been an edition of the Psalms in Hebrew, Greek, Arabic, and Aramaic, published in Genoa in 1516, shortly after the discoveries of Christopher Columbus, which are referred to in a note on Psalm 19:4). This oriental predecessor to the European polyglot editions provided the Psalms in Hebrew, Greek, the Syrohexapla, and Arabic (the use of the Syrohexapla makes it virtually certain that the compiler was Syrian Orthodox).[28] In the manuscript (probably the compiler's autograph, today in the Cambridge University

---

[27] On this revision see my "A neglected revision of the Peshitta Psalter," in C. McCarthy and J. F. Healey (eds.), *Biblical and Near Eastern Essays. Studies in Honour of Kevin J. Cathcart* (JSOT Supplement 375; London, 2004), 131–42.

[28] For this manuscript (Cambridge, Or. 729), see my "A fourteenth-century polyglot Psalter," in G. E. Kadish and G. E. Freedman (eds.), *Studies in Philology in Honour of R. J. Williams* (Toronto, 1982), 1–15.

Library) the Hebrew text is given with both vocalization and accent signs, while the Syrohexapla column is provided with a number of interlinear glosses which bring the Syriac translation into closer line with the Hebrew. What makes this polyglot Psalter unique is the purely scholarly concern of its compiler, and one would dearly like to know who he was.

It is very possible that the idea of producing this academic edition of the Psalter in four languages was taken from some polyglot lectionary texts in use in monasteries in Egypt at about the same time. One such manuscript is again a Psalter, this time in five different languages, Ethiopic, Syriac, Coptic (Bohairic), Arabic, and Armenian. A note at the end informs us that it belonged to "the Syrian Orthodox priest Salib,"[29] who may well be the same person as the Salib of Deir al-Surian who had another such polyglot manuscript, this time with the Epistles of St. Paul, copied by "Yuhanna, the Syrian Orthodox from the town of Amid." A small number of such manuscripts survives, and often they are fragmentary. Since some of them contain lectionary indications it is likely that they were made for practical use in the monasteries of the Wadi Natrun where it is known that monks from many different linguistic backgrounds lived in the thirteenth and fourteenth centuries.

A very much earlier manuscript, probably of the ninth century, contains the Psalter in three languages, Greek, Syriac (Syrohexapla), and Arabic.[30]

Bilingual Syriac biblical manuscripts are rather more commonly found, and normally the second language is Arabic (it is striking that there are no known bilingual biblical manuscripts providing just Syriac and Greek).[31] Although bilingual manuscripts normally present the two languages side by side, in some biblical fragments from Central Asia a different arrangement is found: here Syriac and a translation into Sogdian are given in alternate lines. Sogdian, an Iranian language, was an important literary language of Central Asia in the second half of the first millennium AD, and a

---

[29] The manuscript is Rome (Vatican Library), Barberini Or.2.

[30] See N. Pigulevskaya, "Greko-Siro-Arabskaya Rukopis IX v.," *Palestinskij Sbornik* 1(63) (1954), 59–90 (with photographs).

[31] A rare example of a bilingual, Greek-Syriac, liturgical manuscript is to be found among the "New Finds" at St. Catherine's Monastery, Sinai (Greek ms X239, Liturgy of St John Chrysostom, 12th/13th century), for which see Holy Monastery and Archdiocese of Sinai, *The New Finds of Sinai* (Athens, 1999), 224 (the catalogue of the Greek manuscripts is by P. G. Nicolopoulos).

considerable number of Christian texts, almost all translated from Syriac, were found at Bulayiq, to the north of Turfan in Chinese Turkestan.[32]

TRANSLATIONS OF THE SYRIAC BIBLE INTO OTHER LANGUAGES

Early Translations

Translations of parts or the whole of the Syriac Bible have been made into at least half a dozen different languages. Among the earliest to survive are some fragments found in the ruins of an East Syriac monastery at Bulayiq, north of Turfan, in Chinese Turkestan. These contain parts of biblical translations into Middle Persian, Sogdian, and New Persian.[33] Over the course of time the monks of this monastery evidently used a sequence of different Iranian languages, Middle Persian (Pahlavi), Sogdian, and then New Persian.

It is very likely that a translation of at least the New Testament and Psalms will have been available in Middle Persian by the sixth century, since Middle Persian was a significant literary language of many Christians in the late Sasanian Empire. The only very small fragment to survive contains Psalms 94–99, 118, 121–36, accompanied by the antiphons (*qanone*) composed by Mar Aba in the mid-sixth century.

Among the Sogdian fragments of biblical texts are parts of the Psalter, in which the first verse of each psalm is given in Syriac as well. For the New Testament in Sogdian, all the fragments are from lectionary manuscripts, either of the Gospels, or of the Pauline Epistles. In one Gospel lectionary the opening words of each lection are likewise given in Syriac, and the rubrics also are in Syriac. The other lectionary manuscripts are all bilingual, Syriac and Sogdian.

---

[32] For these, see *The Hidden Pearl*, II, chapter 6.

[33] Middle Persian: F. C. Andreas and K. Barr, "Bruchstücke einer Pehlevi-Übersetzung der Psalmen," *Sitzungsberichte der preussischen Akademie der Wissenschaften* 1933, 91–152; P. Gignoux, "L'Auteur de la version Pehlevie du Psautier serait-il nestorien?," in F. Graffin (ed.), *Mémorial Mgr Gabriel Khouri-Sarkis* (Louvain, 1969), 231–42. Sogdian: M. Schwartz, "Sogdian fragments of the Book of Psalms," *Altorientalische Forschungen* 1 (1974), 257–61; and for New Testament texts, see B. M. Metzger, *Early Versions of the New Testament* (Oxford, 1977), 279–81. New Persian: F. W. K. Müller, "Ein syr.-persisches Psalmenbruchstück aus Chinesisch-Turkestan," in *Festschrift Eduard Sachau* (Berlin, 1915), 215–22. In general on the Sogdian and Persian translations from Syriac, see the *Encyclopaedia Iranica* 4 (1990), 203, 206–8, 210.

By about the eleventh century the language of the monastery had shifted to New Persian, though Syriac still must still have retained an authoritative place, since the one fragment to survive is bilingual; it contains Psalm 146:5–147:7 (in the Peshitta numbering).

Further manuscripts containing Persian translations made from Syriac belong to later in the Middle Ages. One of these, copied in 1341[34] and containing the Gospels, was employed by Brian Walton in his polyglot edition of the Bible published in London in 1657. Although probably not by design, it thus happens that the earliest Persian translation of the Gospels to appear in a printed form derived ultimately from Syriac, which is entirely appropriate, given the important early role of Syriac Christianity in Persia. An important later translation into Persian is that of a lost Syriac form of the Diatessaron, or harmony of the four Gospels. This was made by a Syrian Orthodox layman, Iwannis ʿIzz al-Din, in Tabriz in the thirteenth century. Although the arrangement of the text may go back to that of Tatian's Diatessaron, the underlying Syriac text had been adapted to the Peshitta, and so had lost the many distinctive readings that were evidently present in Tatian's Diatessaron. The only surviving manuscript of this Persian translation was written in 1547 at Hisn Keph by a Syrian Orthodox priest, Ibrahim son of ʿAbdullah.[35] One wonders whether this might not be the same person as the Ibrahim who wrote out the Lord's Prayer in Persian, using Syriac characters, four years later. The manuscript contains a single illustration, with the symbols of the four evangelists; according to some art historians, this goes back to a very early model.[36]

Translations of parts of the Bible into Arabic go back at least to the eighth century, and quite a number of ninth-century fragmentary manuscripts survive.[37] Though several of these translations are made from Greek, others are certainly from Syriac. One of these, preserved in a manuscript dated 867 containing the Acts of the Apostles and the Epistles,

---

[34] Oxford, Bodleian Library, Poc.241.

[35] Edited by G. Messina, *Diatessaron Persiano* (Rome, 1951). See also P. Joosse, "An introduction to the so-called Persian Diatessaron of Iwannis ʿIzz al-Din of Tabriz: the testimony of John 2:1-11 (the Wedding at Cana)," *Oriens Christianus* 86 (2002), 13–45.

[36] For a discussion, see M. Schapiro, "The miniatures of the Florence Diatessaron," *The Art Bulletin* 55 (1973), 494–531, and K. Nordenfalk, "The Diatessaron miniatures once more," *The Art Bulletin* 55 (1973), 532–46.

[37] A brief guide can be found in Metzger, *Early Versions*, 261–4.

was translated from Syriac by Bishri ibn al-Sirri in Damascus.[38] Bishri added a number of annotations, and some prefaces to certain of the Epistles, and these show clear links with the East Syriac exegetical tradition.[39] Many of the earliest Arabic biblical translations made from Syriac are preserved in manuscripts associated with the monasteries of Mar Saba (near Jerusalem) and St. Catherine, on Mount Sinai.

In the thirteenth century an influential edition of the Gospels in Arabic was made by the Ibn al-'Assal brothers in Egypt; this was based on earlier translations made from Greek, Syriac, and Coptic, thus providing a text that brought together these three different traditions.[40]

Translations from Syriac into Arabic were not always based on the Peshitta. In the ninth century translations of parts of the Syrohexapla are known to have been made by Harit ibn Sinan, and one very early manuscript is preserved which contains Job in Arabic translated from the Syrohexapla,[41] while another contains the Psalms in Greek, Syrohexapla, and Arabic. In the eleventh century the famous biblical and Aristotelian scholar Ibn al-Taiyib translated the Diatessaron from Syriac into Arabic. Unfortunately the Syriac text which he used had already been adapted to the Peshitta, and so this too, like the Persian Diatessaron, turns out to be a very indirect witness to the Diatessaron as produced by Tatian.

In medieval sources there are occasional references to interaction between Jewish and Syriac Christian scholars on problems in the biblical text. This seems to have occurred especially in the ninth century, when Hebrew sources record contact between Karaite scholars and named Syriac scholars who can actually be identified from Syriac sources: one was the Syrian Orthodox author Nonnos of Nisibis, and the other, the East Syriac bishop of Uqbara, Isho'zkha.[42] As far as is known, this did not lead to any borrowing yet of Old Testament extra-canonical texts available in Syriac, but no longer in Hebrew (though it has been suggested that the ending of

---

[38] Edited, with English translation, by H. Staal, *Mount Sinai Arabic Codex 151* (CSCO Scr. Arab. 40–43; Louvain, 1983–4).

[39] For this aspect, see my "A neglected witness to the East Syriac New Testament Commentary tradition: Sinai Arabic ms 151," in R. Ebied and H. Teule (eds.), *Studies on the Christian Arabic Heritage* (Eastern Christian Studies 5; Leuven, 2004), 205–15.

[40] For this revision, see K. Samir, "La version arabe des évangiles d'al Assad ibn al-'Assal," *Parole de l'Orient* 19 (1994), 441–551.

[41] Edited by W. de Baudissin, *Translationis antiquae arabicae libri Jobi* (Leipzig, 1870).

[42] See my "Jewish traditions in Syriac sources," *Journal of Jewish Studies* 30 (1979), 230 [repr. in my *Studies in Syriac Christianity* (Aldershot, 1992), Chapter 4)].

Bar Sira (Ecclesiasticus) in the Hebrew fragments preserved in the Cairo Geniza has been retroverted from Syriac). It appears, however, that this sort of borrowing did take place a few centuries later. The most striking case concerns the book of Proverbs, whose Syriac text definitely underlies the medieval Jewish Aramaic Targum of that book. It may also be that the Peshitta Tobit is the source for the Jewish Aramaic translation of that book. In any case it is certain that Nahmanides, the great thirteenth-century Jewish scholar of Gerona, took an interest in books of the Apocrypha in Syriac.[43]

The European Renaissance and Reformation both fostered an interest amongst scholars in the Syriac Bible. Although the first printed edition of the Syriac New Testament, of 1555, did not contain a Latin translation, the next two editions did. The earlier of these two Latin translations to appear was published in Geneva in 1569, and the edition was dedicated to Queen Elizabeth of England. The Latin translation was the work of the Protestant scholar Immanuel Tremellius. The second Latin translation, to be found in the polyglot New Testament published in Antwerp in 1571, was the work of Guy le Fèvre de la Boderie (Boderianus). These Latin translations were frequently reprinted in subsequent years.

Modern Syriac

The earliest translation of any part of the Bible from Classical into Modern Syriac seems to have been of the Gospels, and a manuscript of this, dated 1769, once belonged to the library of the American Mission in Urmi, but (like most of that collection) it was probably destroyed during the First World War. It is possible, however, that two manuscripts, written in the 1880s and now in the United States, are copies of this text, and it may also turn out that it was the basis of an edition of the Gospels published by the Mission in 1873. In all three manuscripts the translation is said to have been made by Israel of Alqosh, this may be the Israel who died around 1611 and is the first known author of poems written in Modern Syriac.

One of the main concerns of the American missionaries in Urmi was to produce translations of the Bible into Modern Syriac. When they first arrived there in 1834 there was no local tradition of writing in the spoken language, and so it was some years before they were in a position to print any such translation. There was, moreover, an initial major decision to take: was the translation to be from Hebrew (for the Old Testament) and from Greek (for the New), or was the Peshitta, the traditional biblical text of the

[43] See M.Weitzman, *The Syriac Version of the Old Testament* (Cambridge, 1999), 161.

Syriac Churches, to be used?[44] On this point there was a difference of opinion between the American Board of Commissioners for Foreign Missions in the United States (who wanted it to be from Hebrew and Greek) and the missionaries themselves in Urmi, who pointed out that local need was for a translation from the Syriac Peshitta. For the New Testament, which was published in 1846, a compromise that favoured the missionaries was reached: the Modern Syriac was translated from the Peshitta (and was printed alongside the Peshitta), but any variations in the Greek were noted at the bottom of the page. In a second edition, in 1854, the same pattern was adopted, although now the Peshitta was no longer given as well. A radical change took place in the edition of 1864, this time printed in the United States: now the American Board of Commissioners were able to see to it that their views were put into practice. Accordingly, in this edition the Greek readings of the footnotes were placed in the text, and in this way any distinctive readings of the Peshitta were effectively removed. Unfortunately it is this edition, now based on the Greek, rather than on the Peshitta, which has been the basis of all the many reprints of the New Testament in Modern Syriac.

In the case of the Old Testament in Modern Syriac (published by the American Mission in Urmi in 1852) the views of the American Board of Commissioners prevailed from the first, and this translation was done from Hebrew.

A separate translation of the Gospels and Acts, made from the Peshitta into the Urmi dialect of Modern Syriac, was published by the Lazarist Mission in that town in 1877. In this edition the Peshitta is printed as well, and indeed is given the greater prominence, since the Modern Syriac translation is printed in a smaller type face.

A translation of the Gospel of Mark into the Iraqi form of Modern Syriac was published in Baghdad in 1991, together with detailed annotation (in Arabic). Though use has been made of the Greek, the translation is largely based on the Peshitta. An edition, by Jacob O. Yasso, of all four Gospels in Modern Syriac in transcription has also been produced, and was published by the Aramaic Bible Society in 1994; this has made use of both the Peshitta and the Greek text.

Although the practice of oral translation from Classical Syriac into another Modern Syriac dialect, Turoyo, is probably quite old, it was not

---

[44] For the following, see my "Translating the New Testament into Syriac (Classical and Modern)," in J. Krasovec (ed.), *Interpretation of the Bible* (Ljubljana/Sheffield, 1998), 378–83.

until the late-nineteenth century that this was ever put into writing. A printed edition of the Gospels in Turoyo, translated from the Peshitta, was published in 1995 by the American Bible Society, with the commendation of the Syrian Orthodox Patriarch, Ignatius Zakka I.

English

Some English translations of parts of the Syriac Bible were already made in the nineteenth century. A translation of the Syriac New Testament, by James Murdock (1776–1856), was published in Boston in 1851, and this was followed by one of the Psalms, by A. Oliver, in 1861, also published in Boston. It seems likely that the interest in undertaking this had been stimulated by the activities of the American mission to the Church of the East in Urmi. Murdock sent a copy of his translation to the missionaries in Urmi, who showed it to Mar Yuhannan, a bishop of the Church of the East with whom they were working. Mar Yuhannan was evidently very pleased with the work and sent Murdock a letter in Syriac full of praise. In an appendix Murdock gave a list of the lections, as they appeared in the two London editions of the Peshitta he had been using (1816, 1826; in the latter several lections for the saints and the departed were tacitly dropped by the publishers, The British and Foreign Bible Society).

Another, anonymous, English translation of the Peshitta New Testament was published in London in 1876, accompanied by the Syriac text, and a further one, of just the Epistles, appeared in 1890, the work of W. Norton.

All these versions are based on standard editions of the Peshitta New Testament where the books absent from the original Peshitta canon had been supplied from other sources (normally the so-called "Pococke" Epistles, and the Harklean Apocalypse). When William Cureton published (in 1858) the first known manuscript of the Old Syriac Gospels he accompanied it with an English translation, but this has now been superseded by the excellent re-edition of the text with a facing English translation by the great biblical scholar F. C. Burkitt.

The only complete translation of the Peshitta Bible, including the Old Testament as well, is that of G. M. Lamsa, first published in 1933, and since then frequently reprinted.

Apart from Burkitt's translation of the Old Syriac Gospels none of these English versions is very satisfactory, and that by Lamsa, in particular, is marred by a number of idiosyncratic interpretations. Currently the Peshitta Institute in Leiden in planning to produce an English translation of the Peshitta Old Testament, based on the text of their critical edition.

Malayalam

The earliest printed translation of any part of the Syriac Bible into Malayalam was one of the Gospels, published in Bombay in 1811. The translation was the work of a certain Timapay Pillay and a priest named Philippos. It seems that the undertaking had originally been suggested by Dr Claudius Buchanan to Mar Dionysius. Just under a century later, a Malayalam translation of the Gospel of Matthew, made by Konatt Matthan Malpan, on the basis of the British and Foreign Bible Society's edition of the Peshitta, was published in Kottayam in 1908.

A number of translations from the Syriac Peshitta into Malayalam were made by Fr. Emmanuel Andumalil (Manikkathanar), T.O.C.D., and published by St. Joseph's Press, Mannanam: Ecclesiasticus (1926), Proverbs (1928), Gospels (1935), New Testament (1938, 1940 and often reprinted), and Tobit (1941). The same press also published Malayalam translations of some other books of the Peshitta made by other scholars (the Psalms, 1940, and Joshua and Ruth). A separate translation of the Psalms, by Fr. Ralph, C.M.I., was subsequently published in Cochin.

A new Malayalam translation of the Peshitta New Testament, the work mainly of Dr. Thomas Kayalaparampil, was published by the St. Thomas Seminary, Vadavathor (Kottayam), in 1987.

The most recent Malayalam translation from the Peshitta is of the entire Bible. This was published in Kottayam in 1997, and is the work of Fr. Mathew Uppani, C.M.I. Although the translation was based on the Mosul edition, the ordering of the books is different in several respects, as will readily be seen by comparing the following list with that for the Mosul edition, given earlier in the chapter:

Pentateuch
Joshua
Judges
1-2 Samuel
1-2 Kings
Isaiah
Jeremiah
Lamentations
Letter of Jeremiah
Ezekiel
2 Baruch
Daniel (including Susanna and Bel)
XII Prophets

1-2 Chronicles
Ezra
Nehemiah
Ruth
Esther (including the extra chapters)
Judith
Tobit
1-2 Maccabees
Job
Psalms
Proverbs
Qohelet
Song
Wisdom
Bar Sira

The sequence of books in the New Testament, on the other hand, follows the standard ordering, rather than the distinctive Peshitta order, with the major Catholic Epistles following immediately after Acts.

TABLE 9:
Translations from the Peshitta

ca. 6th cent.	Middle Persian (fragments only survive)
ca. 8th–11th cent.	Sogdian (fragments only survive)
ca. 9th cent. onwards	Arabic
11th cent.	New Persian (fragments only survive)
16th cent.	Latin
17th cent.	Modern Syriac (Gospel lections only)
19th/20th cent.	Modern Syriac (New Testament) English (parts only) Malayalam

SELECT BIBLIOGRAPHY

I. EDITIONS

(1) Entire Bible (Peshitta)

G. Sionita (Paris Polyglot, 1645)
B. Walton (London Polyglot, 1657)
S. Lee (1823) > United Bible Societies (1979, + Apocrypha)
Urmia edition (1852) > Joseph de Qelayta/Trinitarian Bible Society (1913)
Mosul edition (1887–92) > Beirut (1951)

(2) Old Testament

(a) Peshitta

Critical edition of the Peshitta, based on the oldest manuscripts (Leiden Peshitta Project, *Vetus Testamentum Syriace*):
Sample Edition [Cant., Tobit, IV Ezra] (1966).
I.1, Genesis – Exodus (1977).
I.2 & II.1b, Leviticus, Deuteronomy, Joshua (1991).
II.1a, Job (1982).
II.2, Judges, Sam. (1978).
II.3, Psalms (1980).
II.4, Kings (1976).
II.5, Proverbs, Wisdom, Qohelet (Ecclesiastes), Song of Songs (1979).
III.1, Isaiah (1987).
III.3, Ezekiel (1985).
III.4, XII Prophets, Daniel (1980).
IV.2, Chronicles (1998).
IV.3, Apocalypse of Baruch, IV Ezra (Apocalypse of Ezra) (1973).

IV.6, Odes [*Teshbhotho*], Prayer of Manasseh, Apocryphal Psalms
(Pss 151–155), Psalms of Solomon, Tobit, 1(3) Ezra (1972).
Other critical editions:
Pentateuch (W. Barnes, Cambridge, 1914).
Psalms (W. Barnes, Cambridge, 1904).
Lamentations (B. Albrektson, Lund, 1963).
Wisdom of Solomon (J. A. Emerton, Leiden, 1959).
Ben Sira (F. Vattioni, Naples, 1968; and N. Calduch-Benages,
J. Ferrer and J. Liesen, Estella (Navarra), 2003).
Apocrypha (P. de Lagarde, London, 1861).

(b) Syro-Hexapla (Shab'in 'the Seventy')

A. Ceriani, *Codex Syro-Hexaplaris Ambrosianus photographice editus*
(Monumenta Sacra et Profana VII; Milan,1874).
P. de Lagarde, *Bibliothecae Syriacae…quae ad philologiam sacram pertinent*
(Göttingen, 1892).
W. Baars, *New Syro-Hexaplaric Texts* (Leiden, 1968).
A. Vööbus, *The Pentateuch in the Version of the Syro-Hexapla* (CSCO
Subs. 45, 1975).
A. Vööbus, *The Book of Isaiah in the Version of the Syro-Hexapla* (CSCO
Subs. 68, 1983).
R. J. Hiebert, *The Syrohexapla Psalter* (Atlanta, 1989).

(c) 'Syro-Lucianic'/Philoxenian

A. Ceriani, in *Monumenta Sacra et Profana* V.1 (Milan, 1868).
(For this version see G. Jenkins, *The Old Testament Quotations of
Philoxenus* (CSCO Subs. 84; 1989).

(d) Jacob of Edessa (the surviving texts are listed by W. Baars in *Vetus
Testamentum* 18 (1968), 548–54)

A. Ceriani, in *Monumenta Sacra et Profana* II.1 (Milan, 1963) [Genesis],
and V.1 (1868) [Isaiah].
A. Salvesen, *The Books of Samuel in the Syriac Version of Jacob of Edessa*
(MPIL 10; Leiden, 1999).
(For this version see also R. J. Saley, *The Samuel Manuscript of Jacob of
Edessa* (MPIL 9; Leiden, 1998).

(e) Christian Palestinian Aramaic

C. Müller-Kessler and M. Sokoloff, *A Corpus of Christian Palestinian
Aramaic, I. Old Testament and Apocrypha* (Groningen, 1997). This
replaces earlier editions.

(3) New Testament

(a) Diatessaron (excerpted from Ephrem's Commentary (ed. Leloir, 1963):

    I. Ortiz de Urbina, *Vetus Evangelium Syrorum; Diatessaron Tatiani* (Madrid, 1967).

(b) Old Syriac, Peshitta and Harclean Gospels:

    G. A. Kiraz, *Comparative Edition of the Syriac Gospels* (4 vols, Leiden, 1996).

(c) Old Syriac Gospels

    F. C. Burkitt, *Evangelion da-Mepharreshe I–II* (1904; repr. Piscataway NJ, 2003) - based on the Curetonian manuscript (a further folio of the Curetonian with Luke 16 is published by D. McConaughy in *Biblica* 68 (1987), 85–8).

    A. S. Lewis, *The Old Syriac Gospels* (1910; repr. Piscataway NJ, 2005) - based on the Sinai manuscript.

    (For quotations from Acts see J. Kerschensteiner in *Biblica* 45 (1964), 63–74, and for those from the Pauline Epistles, see his *Der altsyrische Paulustext* (CSCO Subs. 37; 1970).

(d) Peshitta

Whole NT:

    - British and Foreign Bible Society (1920 and reprints).

    - United Bible Society (1979; this edition reproduces Lee (1823) in the New as well as the Old Testament; in reprints from 1988 onwards, however, the New Testament is reproduced from the NT from British and Foreign Bible Society edition).

    - *The Aramaic New Testament* (The Way International, New Knoxville, 1983). [Estrangelo script]

Gospels:

    - P. E. Pusey and G. H. Gwilliam, *Tetraevangelium Syriacum* (Oxford, 1901). This is a critical edition, using the oldest manuscripts; it is provided with a facing Latin translation.

    - Mor Gabriel edition, Pshitto of Mardin (Istanbul, 1998).

Epistles:

    - B. Aland and A. Juckel, *Das Neue Testament in syrischer Überlieferung*, I (Berlin, 1986) [Major Catholic Epistles]; II.1

(1991) [Romans, I Corinthians]; II.2 (1995) [II Corinthians –
Colosians]; II.3 (2002) [I Thessalonians – Hebrews].

(e) Sixth-Century Translation (Philoxenian?)

Minor Catholic Epistles ('Pococke Epistles'):
- J. Gwynn, *Remnants of Later Syriac Versions* (1909; repr.
  Piscataway NJ, 2005);

Apocalypse ('Crawford Apocalypse'):
- J. Gwynn, *The Apocalypse of St John in a Syriac Version hitherto
  unknown* (1897; reprint Piscataway NJ, 2005).

(f) Harklean

Whole NT:
- J. White, *Sacrorum Evangeliorum versio Syriaca Philoxeniana* [!, in fact
  Harclean]   (Oxford,   1778);   *Actuum   Apostolorum   et
  Epistolarum…versio Syriaca Philoxeniana* [!, in fact Harklean]
  (Oxford, 1799/1803).

Gospels:
- G. Kiraz, *Comparative Edition of the Syriac Gospels* (4 vols, Leiden,
  1996).

Epistles:
- B. Aland and A. Juckel, *Das NT in syrischer Überlieferung* [see
  under (c)].

Apocalypse:
- A. Vööbus, *The Apocalypse in the Harklean Version* (CSCO Subs.
  56, 1978)

(g) Christian Palestinian Aramaic

C. Müller-Kessler and M. Sokoloff, *A Corpus of Christian Palestinian
Aramaic.* IIA, IIB, The New Testament (Groningen,1998).

A. Lewis and M. Gibson, *The Palestinian Syriac Lectionary of the Gospels*
(1899).

II. TOOLS

(1) Lists of Manuscripts

List of Old Testament Peshitta Manuscripts (Peshitta Institute, Leiden, 1961)

J. T. Clemons, *An index of Syriac manuscripts containing the Epistles and
Apocalypse* (Studies and Documents 33, 1968).

J. D. Thomas, 'A list of manuscripts containing the Harclean Syriac version of the New Testament', *Theological Review, Near Eastern School of Theology* 2:2 (1979), 26–32.

(2) Concordances

(a) Old Testament:

P. G. Borbone and F. Mandracci, *Concordanze del testo siriaco di Osea* (Memorie dell'Accademi delle Scienze di Torino, V.11.1–4; 1987).

K. D. Jenner and P. G. Borbone, *A Concordance to the Old Testament in Syriac*, I. *The Pentateuch* (Leiden, 1997).

W. Strothmann, *Konkordanz zur syrischen Bibel. Der Pentateuch* (GOFS 26; Wiesbaden, 1986); *Die Propheten* (GOFS 25; 1984), 4 vols. each; *Die Mautbe* (GOFS 33; 1995), 6 vols.

————, *Konkordanz des syrischen Koheletbuches nach der Peschitta und der Syrohexapla* (GOFS 4; Wiesbaden, 1973)

————, *Wörtverzeichnis der apokryphen-deuterokanonischen Schriften des AT* (GOFS 27; Wiesbaden, 1988)

N. Sprenger, *Konkordanz zum syrischem Psalter* (GOFS 10; Wiesbaden, 1976)

M. Winter, *A Concordance to the Peshitta Version of Ben Sira* (Leiden, 1976)

(b) New Testament:

Anon., *The Concordance to the Peshitta Version of the Aramaic NT* (New Knoxville, 1985) [In fact a word list, not a concordance].

G. Kiraz, *A Computer-Generated Concordance to the Syriac New Testament* (Leiden, 1993), 6 vols.

J. Lund, *The Old Syriac Gospel of the Distinct Evangelists. A Key-Word-in-Context Concordance* (Piscataway NJ, 2004), 3 vols.

(c) Dictionaries

T. Falla, *A Key to the Peshitta Gospels*, I [*alaph* to *dalath*] (Leiden, 1991); II [*he* to *yudh*] (Leiden, 2000).

W. Jennings, *Lexicon to the Syriac New Testament* (Oxford, 1926)

G. Kiraz, *Lexical Tools to the Syriac New Testament* (Sheffield, 1994).

M. Pazzini, *Lessico concordanziale del Nuovo Testamento Siriaco* (Jerusalem, 2004).

C. Schaaf, *Lexicon syriacum concordantiale* (Leiden, 1709).

(d) Bibliographies

(I) Old Testament:

P. B. Dirksen, *An Annotated Bibliography of the Peshitta Old Testament* (MPI 5; 1989) [there is a supplement in P. Dirksen and A. van der Kooij, *The Peshitta as a Translation* (Leiden, 1995), 221–36].

For Syro-hexapla and OT books translated from Greek:

S. P. Brock, C. T. Fritsch and S. Jellicoe, *A Classified Bibliography of the Septuagint* (Leiden, 1973), 189–94, and C. Dogniez, *Bibliography of the Septuagint 1970–1993* (Leiden, 1995), 303–6.

(II) New Testament:

No specialized bibliography exists, but materials can fairly readily be found in the following:

C. Moss, *Catalogue of Syriac printed books and related literature in the British Museum* (London, 1962), and S.P. Brock, *Syriac Studies: a Classified Bibliography, 1960–1990* (Kaslik, 1996), 43–62, with supplements for 1991–1995 in *Parole de l'Orient* 23 (1998), 261–67, and for 1996–2000 in *Parole de l'Orient* 29 (2004), 286–94.

III. TRANSLATIONS

F. C. Burkitt, - see above, 3 (c).

A. Salvesen, - see above, 2 (d).

The following need to be used with caution:

G. M. Lamsa (Philadelphia, 1957; London, 1961 and reprints).

J. Murdock (Boston/London, 1851; repr. (from 1893 edn.) Piscataway NJ, 2001). [NT]

W. Norton (London, 1890). [NT Epistles]

A. Oliver (Boston, 1861). [Psalms]

J. Wilson (Piscataway NJ, 2002). [Old Syriac Gospels]

For the proposed annotated English translation of the Peshitta, see:

K. D. Jenner, A. Salvesen, R. B. Ter Haar Romeny, W. T. van Peursen, 'The new English Annotated Translation of the Syriac Bible', *Aramaic Studies* 2 (2004), 85–106.

R. B. ter Haar Romeny, 'Choosing a textual basis for the New English Annotated translation of the Syriac Bible', *Aramaic Studies* 3 (2005), 167–86.

IV. STUDIES

(1) General Surveys: Old Testament And New Testament In Syriac

B. Aland and S. P. Brock, in *Theologische Realenzyklopädie* 6 (1980), 181–96.

S. P. Brock, in *Anchor Dictionary of the Bible* 6 (1992), 794–9.

M. van Esbroeck, in J. Krašovec (ed.), *Interpretation of the Bible* (Sheffield/Ljubljana, 1998), 480–502.

C. van Puyvelde, in *Dictionnaire de la Bible, Supplément* 6 (1960), 834–84.

A. Vööbus, in *The Interpreter's Dictionary of the Bible, Supplemenary Volume* (Abingdon, 1976~, 848–54.

(2) Old Testament: General Studies

S. P. Brock, 'The Peshitta Old Testament: between Judaism and Christianity', *Cristianesimo nella Storia* 19 (1998), 483–502.

P. Dirksen, *La Peshitta dell'Antico Testamento* (Brescia, 1993).

———, 'The Old Testament Peshitta: its early text and history', in M. J. Mulder (ed.), *Miqra* (Compendia Rerum Iudaicarum ad Novum Testamentum 2:1, 1988), 255–97.

P. Dirksen and M. Mulder (eds.), *The Peshitta, its Early Text and History* (MPI 4; Leiden, 1988).

P. Dirksen and A. van der Kooij (eds.), *The Peshitta as a Translation* (MPI 8; Leiden, 1995).

M. D. Koster, 'The Copernican revolution in the study of the origins of the Peshitta', in P. V. M. Flesher (ed.), *Targum and Peshitta* (Atlanta, 1998), 15–54.

———, 'A new introduction to the Peshitta of the Old Testament', *Aramaic Studies* 1 (2003), 211–46. [On Weitzman, *The Syriac Version of the OT*].

R. A. Taylor, 'The Syriac Old Testament in recent research', *Journal of the Aramaic Bible* 2 (2000), 119–139.

B. Ter Haar Romeny, 'The Peshitta and its rivals', *The Harp* (SEERI) 11/12 (1999), 21–31. [On Syriac views of origins of the Peshitta OT].

———, 'The Syriac versions of the Old Testament', in *Nos sources: arts et littérature syriaques* (Centre d'Études et de Recherches Orientales, Antelias, 2005), 75–105.

M. Weitzman, *The Syriac Version of the Old Testament. An Introduction* (Cambridge, 1999).

————, (ed. A. Rapoport Albert and G. Greenberg), *From Judaism to Christianity: Studies in the Hebrew and Syriac Bibles* (Sheffield, 1999). [Collected articles]

(3) Old Testament: Particular Books/Topics

W. Bloemendaal, *The Headings of the Psalms in the East Syrian Church* (Leiden, 1960).

S. P. Brock, 'A Palestinian Targum feature in Syriac', *Journal of Jewish Studies* 46 (1995), 271–82.

————, 'Text divisions in the Syriac translations of Isaiah', in A. Rapoport-Albert and G. Greenberg (eds.), *Biblical Hebrew, Biblical Texts. Essays in Memory of M. P. Weitzman* (Sheffield, 2001), 200–221.

P. B. Dirksen, *The Transmission of the Text in the Peshitta Manuscripts of the Book of Judges* (MPI 1; Leiden, 1972).

P. V. M. Flesher (ed.), *Targum and Peshitta* (Atlanta, 1998).

A. Gelston, *The Peshitta of the Twelve Prophets* (Oxford, 1987).

G. Greenberg, *Translation Technique in the Peshitta to Jeremiah* (MPIL 13; Leiden, 2002).

K. D. Jenner, 'The Syriac Daniel', in J. J. Collins and P. W. Gentry (eds.), *The Book of Daniel. Composition and Reception* (Suppl. to Vetus Testamentum 83:2 (2001), 608–37.

M. D. Koster, *The Peshitta of Exodus* (Assen, 1977).

D. J. Lane, *The Peshitta of Leviticus* (MPI 6; Leiden, 1994).

Y. Maori, *The Peshitta Version of the Pentateuch and its Relation to the Sources of Jewish Exegesis* (Jerusalem, 1998) [in Hebrew].

C. E. Morrison, *The Character of the Syriac Version of the First Book of Samuel* (MPIL 11; Leiden, 2001).

M. D. Nelson, *The Syriac Version of the Wisdom of Ben Sira compared to the Greek and Hebrew Materials* (SBL Dissertation Series 107; 1988).

R. J. Owens, *The Genesis and Exodus Citations of Aphrahat the Persian Sage* (MPI 3; Leiden, 1983).

R. Sörries, *Die syrische Bibel von Paris BN syr. 341* [8a1]. *Eine fruhchristliche Bilderhandschrift aus dem 6. Jhdt.* (Wiesbaden, 1991).

H. M. Szpek, *Translation Technique in the Peshitta to Job* (SBL Dissertation Series 137; 1992).

R. A. Taylor, *The Peshitta of Daniel* (MPI 7; Leiden, 1994).

J. P. M. van der Ploeg, *The Book of Judith* (Moran Etho 3; Kottayam, 1991). [A version of uncertain origin].

A. Vööbus, *Peschitta und Targumim des Pentatuechs* (Stockholm, 1958).

P. J. Williams, *Studies in the Syntax of the Peshitta of I Kings* (MPIL 12; Leiden, 2001).

M. A. Zipor, *The Peshitta Version of Leviticus, with a Commentary* (Jerusalem, 2003) [in Hebrew].

(4) New Testament: General Studies

T. Baarda, 'The Syriac versions of the New Testament', in B. D. Ehrman and M. W. Holmes (eds.), *The Text of the New Testament in Contemporary Research* (Grand Rapids, 1995), 97–112.

M. Black, 'The Syriac versional evidence', in K. Aland (ed.), *Die alten Übersetzungen des NT* (Berlin, 1972), 120–159.

S. P. Brock, 'Translating the New Testament into Syriac (Classical and Modern)', in J. Krašovec (ed.), *Interpretation of the Bible* (Sheffield/ Ljubljana, 1998), 371–385.

F. C. Burkitt, *Early Eastern Christianity* (1904; repr. Piscataway NJ, 2004), Ch. 2 [Influential but largely outdated now].

J. Joosten, *The Syriac Language of the Peshitta and Old Syriac Versions of Matthew* (1996).

A. Juckel, 'Die Peschitta des Neuen Testaments - gemeinsame Erbe der Syrischen Kirchen', in *Nos sources: arts et littérature syriaques* (Centre d'Études et de Recherches Orientales, Antelias, 2005), 107–42.

K. Luke, 'The Syriac versions of the New Testament', *Bible Bhashyam* 19 (1993), 300–14; 20 (1994), 124–38.

J. P. Lyon, *Syriac Gospel translations* (CSCO Subs. 88, 1994).

B. M. Metzger, *The Early Versions of the New Testament* (Oxford, 1977), Ch. 1.

A. Vööbus, *Studies in the History of the Gospel Text in Syriac, I–II* (CSCO Subs. 3, 79; 1951, 1987)

———, *Early Versions of the New Testament* (1954)

P. J. Williams, *Early Syriac Translation Technique and the Textual Criticism of the Greek Gospels* (Piscataway NJ, 2004).

(5) New Testament: Particular Books/Topics

T. Baarda, *Essays on the Diatessaron* (Kampen, 1994).

S. P. Brock, 'The resolution of the Philoxenian/Harklean problem', in *Essays in Honour of B. M. Metzger* (Oxford, 1981), 325–343.

———, 'The lost Old Syriac at Luke 1:35 and the earliest Syriac terms for the incarnation', in W. Petersen (ed.), *Gospel Traditions in the Second Century* (Notre Dame, 1989), 117–31.

————, 'The Gates/Bars of Sheol revisited', in W. L. Petersen and others (eds.), *Sayings of Jesus: canonical and uncanonical* (Supplements to Novum Testamentum 89, 1997), 7–24.

————, 'Hebrews 2:9b in Syriac tradition', *Novum Testamentum* 27 (1985), 236–44.

J. Joosten, 'West Aramaic elements in the Old Syriac and Peshitta Gospels', *JBL* 110 (1991), 271–289.

C. V. Malzoni, *Jesus: Messias e Vivificador do Mundo. Jo 4, 1–42 na Antiga Tradicao Siriaca* (Cahiers de la Revue Biblique 59; 2005).

W. Petersen, *Tatian's Diatessaron. Its Creation, Dissemination, Significance and History in Scholarship* (Leiden, 1994).

————, 'Diatessaron', in *Anchor Dictionary of the Bible* 2 (1992), 189–90

V. LECTIONARIES

(1) General Studies

A. Baumstark, *Nichtevangelische syrische Perikopenordningen der ersten Jahrtausends* (1921).

Y. Burns, 'The Greek manuscripts connected by their lection systems with the Palestinian Syriac Gospel Lectionaries', *Studia Biblica* (ed. E. A. Livingstone; Sheffield, 1980), II, 13–28.

A. Desreumaux, 'Les lectionnaires syro-palestiniens', in C.-B. Amphoux (ed.), *La lecture liturgique des Épîtres catholiques dans l'Église ancienne* (Lausanne, 1996), 87–103.

H. Engberding, 'Das Rätsel einer Reihe von 16 Sonntagsepisteln', *Oriens Christianus* 52 (1968), 81–86. [On the Palestinian Syriac Lectionary, ed. A. S. Lewis].

A. Jaubert, 'Une lecture du lavement des pieds au mardi-mercredi saint', *Le Muséon* 79 (1966), 257–86.

K. Jenner, 'Development of Syriac lectionary systems', *The Harp* (SEERI) 10 (1997), 9–24.

————, 'The relation between Biblical text and Lectionary systems in the Eastern Church', in A. Rapoport-Albert and G. Greenberg (eds.), *Biblical Hebrew, Biblical Texts* (Sheffield, 2001), 376–411.

P. Kannookadan, *The East Syrian Lectionary. An Historico-Liturgical Study* (Rome, 1991).

W. Macomber, 'The Chaldean Lectionary system of the Cathedral Church of Kokhe', *Orientalia Christiana Periodica* 33 (1967), 483–516.

B. M. Metzger, 'A comparison of the Palestinian Syriac Lectionary and the Greek Gospel Lectionary', in E. E. Ellis and M. Wilcox (eds.),

Neotestamentica et Semitica: Studies in Honour of Principal M. Black (Edinburgh, 1969), 209–20. [See also the review in *Journal of Theological Studies* 15 (1970), 268–70].

G. Rouwhorst, 'Les lectionnaires syriaques', in C.-B. Amphoux (ed.), *La lecture liturgique des Épîtres catholiques dans l'Église ancienne* (Lausanne, 1996), 105–40.

J-M. Vosté, 'Le Gannat Bussame', *Revue Biblique* 37 (1928), 386–91.

(2) Particular Manuscripts

A. Allgeier, 'Cod. syr. Phillips 1388 und seine ältesten Perikopenmerke', *Oriens Christianus* ns 6 (1916), 147–52. [Gospels].

A. Baumstark, 'Neuerschlossene Urkunden altchristlicher Perikopenordnung des ostaramäischen Sprachgebietes', *Oriens Christianus* 23 (1927), 1–22.

F. C. Burkitt, 'The Early Syriac Lectionary System', *Proceedings of the British Academy* (1923), 301–38. [On British Library, Add. 14528].

———, *The Religion of the Manichees* (Cambridge, 1925), 119–25. [Lections in a 9th-century Sogdian Lectionary from Turfan].

O. Heiming, 'Ein jakobitisches Doppellektionar des Jahres 824 aus Harran in BM Add. 14485 bis 14487', in *Kyriakon. Festschrift J. Quasten* II (Münster, 1970), 368–99.

K. D. Jenner, *De Perikopentitels van de geillustreerde syrische kanselbijbel van Parijs* [= 8a1] (Diss. Leiden, 1993).

A. Merk, 'Das älteste Perikopensystem des Rabbulakodex', *Zeitschrift für Katholische Theologie* 37 (1913), 202–14. [Gospels].

A. Rücker, 'Ein weiterer Zeuge der älteren Perikopenordnung der syrische Jakobiten', *Oriens Christianus* ns 7/8 (1918), 146–53. [Gospels].

A. Vööbus, *The Lectionary of the Monastery of 'Aziza'el in Tur 'Abdin* (CSCO Subs. 73; 1985).

———, *A Syriac Lectionary from the Church of the Forty Martyrs in Mardin* (CSCO Subs. 76; 1986).

(3) Lists of Lections

Mar Aprem, *Nestorian Lectionary and Julian Calendar* (Trichur, 1982).

L. Chidiac, G. Khouri-Sarkis, P. Vermeulen, 'Tableau des péricopes bibliques dans les Églises de langue syriaque', *L'Orient Syrien* 3 (1958), 359–86; 12 (1967), 211–40, 371–88, 525–48.

Mar Cyril Afrem Karim, *Scripture Readings for Sundays and Feast Days according to the Tradition of the Syrian Orthodox Church of Antioch* ([Teaneck, NJ], 2000). [Based on list published by Mar Filoksinos Yuhanon Dolabani, Mardin, 1954].

A. J. Maclean, *East Syrian Daily Offices* (1894; repr. Piscataway NJ, 2003), Appendix.

VI. EXEGESIS (see Part I, Ch. 4–5)

(1) Editions And Translations of the Main Commentaries

In each section authors are listed in chronological order, and from the 5th century onward indication is given whether they belong to the East [E] or West [W] Syriac tradition. Unpublished commentaries are not included.

(a) Old Testament

Ephrem, Comm. on Genesis and Exodus (ed., with Latin tr., R. Tonneau, CSCO Scr. Syri 71–2; 1955); English tr. in E. G. Mathews and J. Amar, *St Ephrem the Syrian. Selected Prose Works* (Washington DC, 1994); and of the Comm. on Exodus in A. Salvesen, *The Exodus Commentary of St Ephrem* (Moran Etho 8; Kottayam 1995).

John the Solitary, Comm. on Qohelet (ed. W. Strothmann, GOFS 30; 1988).

Daniel of Salah [W], Comm. on Psalms (ed., J. Çiçek, Barhebraeus Verlag, 2004; and ed., with English tr., D. G. K. Taylor, CSCO Scr. Syri, forthcoming).

Jacob of Edessa [W], Comm. on the Hexaemeron (ed. J. B. Chabot, CSCO Scr. Syri 43–44; 1927–8); also ed. J. Çiçek, Bar Hebraeus Verlag 1985).

Anonymous (in olim Diarbekir 22) [E], Comm. on Genesis and Exodus 1–9:32 (ed., with French tr., L. van Rompay, CSCO Scr. Syri 205–6; 1986).

Theodore bar Koni [E], Scholia (ed. A. Scher, CSCO Scr. Syri 19, 26; 1910, 1912; French tr., R. Hespel and R. Draguet, CSCO Scr. Syri 187, 188; 1981–2); another recension, ed., with French tr., R. Hespel, CSCO Scr. Syri 193–4; 1983).

Isho' bar Nun [E], Selected Questions on the Pentateuch (ed. + ET, E. G. Clarke, 1962).

Isho'dad of Merv [E], Comm. on the OT (ed., with French tr., C. van den Eynde, CSCO Scr. Syri 67, 75; 80–81; 96–97; 128–9; 146–7; 185–6; 1950–1981).

Anonymous [E], Comm. on Genesis 1–18 (ed. A. Levene, 1951).

Moshe bar Kepha [W], Comm. on the Hexaemeron (German tr., L. Schlimme, GOFS 17; 1977).

————, Comm. on Paradise (Hungarian tr., A. Köver, I. Lukács, M. Pesthy, 2001).

Dionysius bar Salibi [W], Comm. on Qohelet (ed. W. Strothmann, GOFS 31; 1988).

————, Comm. on Psalms 73–82 (ed., with English tr., S. D. Ryan, 2004).

Gannat Bussame [E], Comm. on Lectionary (I, *Adventssonntage*, ed., with German tr., G. J. Reinink, CSCO Scr. Syri, 211–2; 1988).

Bar Hebraeus [W], *Ausar Raze*/Scholia on Gen. – 2 Sam. (ed. + ET M. Sprengling and W. C. Graham, 1931; also ed. (for whole Bible) J. Çiçek, Bar Hebraeus Verlag, 2003).

(b) New Testament

Ephrem, Comm. on the Diatessaron (ed., with Latin tr., L. Leloir, 1963 and 1990; English tr., C. McCarthy, 1993; French tr., L. Leloir, Sources chrétiennes 121; 1966).

Philoxenus [W], Comm. on the Prologue of John (ed., with French tr., A. de Halleux, CSCO Scr. Syri 165–6); 1977.

————, Comm. on Matthew and Luke (ed., with English tr., J. Watt, CSCO Scr. Syri 171–2; 1978).

Isho'dad of Merv [E], Comm. on New Testament (ed., with English tr., M. D. Gibson, *Horae Semiticae* 5–7, 10; 1911–1913).

Moshe bar Kepha [W], Comm. on John (ed., with German tr., L. Schlimme, GOFS 18; 1978).

————, Comm. on Romans (ed., with German tr., J. Reller, GOFS 35; 1994).

Dionysius bar Salibi [W], Comm. on the Gospels, Acts, Cath. Epp., Apoc. (ed., with Latin tr., I. Sedlacek and others, CSCO 15–16; 33,40; 47,60 [Mt – Lk]; 18, 20 [Acts – Apoc.]; 1906–1940; ed. R. Lejoly [Jn], 1975).

Bar Hebraeus [W], Comm. on Gospels (ed., with English tr., W. F. Carr, 1925).

(c) Translations From Greek

Athanasius, Comm. on Psalms (ed., with English tr., R. W. Thomson, CSCO Scr. Syri 167–8; 1977).

Basil, Comm. on the Hexaemeron (ed., with English tr., R. W. Thomson, CSCO Scr. Syri 222–3; 1995).

Cyril of Alexandria, Hom. on Luke (ed. J. B. Chabot, CSCO Scr. Syri 27; 1912; with Latin tr., R. Tonneau, CSCO Scr. Syri 70; 1970).

Theodore of Mopsuestia, Comm. on Psalms 118, 138–148 (ed., with French tr., L. van Rompay, CSCO Scr. Syri 189–90; 1982).

———, Comm. on Qohelet (ed. W. Strothmann, GOFS 28; 1988; cp 29, 1988 for Catena fragments).

———, Comm. on John (ed., with Latin tr., I-M. Vosté, CSCO Scr. Syri 62–63; 1940).

(2) Studies

(a) General Introductions

P. Féghali, 'L'exégèse syriaque', in *Nos sources: arts et littérature syriaques* (Centre d'Études et de Recherches Orientales, Antelias, 2005), 143–76.

J. C. McCullough, 'Early Syriac Commentaries on the New Testament', I–II, *Near East School of Theology* (Beirut), *Theological Review* 5 (1982), 14–33, 79–126.

L. van Rompay, 'The Christian Syriac tradition of interpretation', in M. Sæbø (ed.), *Hebrew Bible/Old Testament*, I.i (Göttingen, 1996), 612–41.

———, 'Development of biblical interpretation in the Syrian Churches of the Middle Ages', in M. Sæbø (ed.), *Hebrew Bible/Old Testament*, I.ii (Göttingen, 2000), 559–577.

(b) On Early Writers

G. Anderson, 'The Cosmic Mountain: Eden and its early interpreters in Syriac Christianity', in G. A. Robbins (ed.), *Genesis 1–3 in the History of Exegesis* (Lewiston NY, 1988), 187–224.

E. Beck, 'Zur Terminologie von Ephrams Bildtheologie', in M. Schmidt (ed.), *Typus Symbol, Allegorie…* (Regensburg, 1982), 329–77.

S. P. Brock, 'Jewish Traditions in Syriac sources', *Journal of Jewish Studies* 30 (1979), 212–32.

J. Frishman and L. van Rompay (eds.), *The Book of Genesis in Jewish and Oriental Christian Interpretation* (Leuven, 1997). [Several contributions are on Syriac topics of relevance].

J. Glenthøj, *Cain and Abel in Syriac and Greek Writers (4th–6th centuries)* (CSCO Subs. 95; 1997).

S. H. Griffith, *'Faith adoring the Mystery', Reading the Bible with St Ephrem the Syrian* (Milwaukee, 1997).

A. Guillaumont, 'Un midrash d'Exode 4, 24–6 chez Aphraate et Éphrem de Nisibe', in R. H. Fischer (ed.), *A Tribute to Arthur Vööbus* (Chicago, 1977), 89–95.

M. Henze, *The Madness of King Nebuchadnezzar* (Leiden, 1999), 143–201 [in early Syriac literature].

T. Kronholm, *Motifs from Genesis 1–11 in the Genuine Hymns of Ephrem the Syrian, with particular reference to the influence of Jewish exegetical tradition* (Lund, 1978).

M. Maas (with contribution by E. G. Mathews), *Exegesis and Empire in the Early Byzantine Mediterranean* (Tübingen, 2003).

C. E. Morrison, 'The reception of the book of Daniel in Aphrahat's Fifth Demonstration, On Wars', *Hugoye* 4:2 (2001).

R. Murray, 'The lance which re-opened Paradise', *Orientalia Christiana Periodica* 39 (1973), 224–34, 491.

———, 'The theory of symbolism in St Ephrem's theology', *Parole de l'Orient* 6/7 (1975/6), 1–20.

———, 'Der Dichter als Exeget: der hl. Ephram und die heutige Exegese', *Zeitschrift für Katholische Theologie 100* (1978), 484–94.

S. Muto, 'Early Syriac hermeneutics', *The Harp* 11/12 (1998/9), 43–65.

A. Salvesen, 'The Exodus Commentary of St Ephrem', *Studia Patristica* 25 (1993), 332–8; cp also *The Harp* 4 (1991), 21–34.

B. Sony, 'La méthode exégétique de Jacques de Saroug', *Parole de l'Orient* 11 (1983), 67–103.

S. S. Taylor, 'Paul and the Persian Sage: some observations on Aphrahat's use of the Pauline Corpus', in C. A. Evans and J. A. Sanders (eds.), *The Function of Scripture in Early Jewish and Christian Tradition* (Sheffield, 1998), 312–31.

R. B. ter Haar Romeny, *A Syrian in Greek Dress. The Use of Greek, Hebrew and Syriac Biblical Texts in Eusebius of Emesa's Commentary on Genesis* (Leuven, 1997).

K. A. Valavanolickal, *The Use of the Gospel Parables in the Writings of Aphrahat and Ephrem* (Frankfurt a/M, 1996).

L. van Rompay, 'L'informateur syrien de Basile de Césarée. À propos de Genèse 1,2', *Orientalia Christiana Periodica* 58 (1992), 145–51.

E. Vergani, 'Isaia 6 nella letteratura siriaca', *Annali di Scienze Religiose* 4 (1999), 287–303; 7 (2002), 169–92.

(c) On Later Writers

(I) Old Testament

M. Albert, 'Les commentaires syriaques sur les Psaumes. Un exemple, le Ps.45', in P. Maraval (ed.), *Le Psautier chez les Pères* (Cahiers de la Biblia Patristica 4; 1994), 255–70.

L. Brade, *Untersuchungen zum Scholienbuch des Theodoros bar Konai* (GOFS 8; 1975).

S. P. Brock, 'Genesis 22 in Syriac tradition', in *Mélanges D. Barthélemy* (Fribourg/Göttingen, 1981), 2–30.

B. Chiesa, 'La tradizione esegetica siriaca', in his *Filologia storica della Bibia ebraica*, I (Brescia, 2000), 109–32.

T. Jansma, 'Investigations into the early Syriac Fathers on Genesis', *Oudtestamentische Studien* 12 (1958), 69–181.

D. Kruisheer, 'Ephrem, Jacob of Edessa and the Monk Severus', in *Symposium Syriacum VII* (Orientalia Christiana Analecta 256; 1998), 599–605.

C. Leonhard, *Ishodad of Merv's Exegesis of the Psalms 119 and 139–147* (CSCO Subs. 107; 2001).

R. Macina, 'L'homme à l'école de Dieu. D'Antioche à Nisibe: profil herméneutique, théologique et kérygmatique du mouvement scholastique nestorien', *Proche Orient Chretien* 32 (1982), 86–124, 263–301; 33 (1983), 39–103.

C. Molenberg, 'An eighth-century manual. Isho' bar Nun's Questions and Answers on the whole text of Scripture as a representative of a genre', in *IV Symposium Syriacum* (Orientalia Christiana Analecta 229; 1987), 45–55.

———, *The Commentary on the Books of the Holy Prophets in a Manuscript in Leningrad. An Epitome of Isho'dad of Merv* (CSCO Subs. 77; 1987).

———, *The Interpreter Interpeted. Isho' bar Nun's selected Questions on the Old Testament* (Diss. Groningen, 1990).

G. J. Reinink, 'Die Textüberlieferung der Gannat Bussame', *Le Muséon* 90 (1977), 103–75. [See also under NT].

————, 'The Lamb on the Tree. Syriac exegesis and anti-Islamic apologetics', in E. Noort and E. Tigchelaar (eds.), *The Sacrifice of Isaac. The Aqedah (Gen. 22) and its Interpretations* (Leiden, 2002), 109–24.

A. Salvesen, 'Did Jacob of Edessa know Hebrew?', in A. Rapoport-Albert and G. Greenberg (eds.), *Biblical Hebrew/Biblical Texts* (Sheffield, 2001), 457–67.

W. Strothmann, 'Das Buch Kohelet und seine syrischen Ausleger', in GOFS 3 (1973), 1890–238.

S. Stroumsa, 'The impact of Syriac tradition on early Judaeo-Arabic Bible exegesis', *Aram* 3 (1991), 83–96.

R. B. ter Haar Romeny, 'Biblical studies in the Church of the East: the case of Catholicos Timothy I', *Studia Patristica* 34 (2001), 503–10.

————, 'The Hebrew and Greek as alternatives to the Syriac version in Isho'dad's Commentary on the Psalms', in A. Rapoport-Albert and G. Greenberg (eds.), *Biblical Hebrew/Biblical Texts* (Sheffield, 2001), 431–56.

————, 'The identity formation of Syrian Orthodox Christians as reflected in two exegetical collections: first soundings', *Parole de l'Orient* 29 (2004), 103–21.

————, 'Question and Answer collections in Syriac literature', in A. Volgers and C. Zamagni (eds.), *Erotapokriseis. Early Christian Question and Answer Literature in Context* (Leuven, 2004), 146–63.

L. van Rompay, 'A hitherto unknown Nestorian Commentary on Gen. and Exod.1–9,32', *Orientalia Lovaniensia Periodica* 5 (1974), 53–78.

————, 'Le commentaire sur Gen. – Exod. 9,32 ... et l'exégèse syrienne orientale du huitième au dixième siècle', *Symposium Syriacum* (Orientalia Christiana Analecta 205, 1978), 113–23.

————, 'La littérature exégétique syriaque et le rapprochement des traditions syrienne orientale et syrienne occidentale', *Parole de l'Orient* 20 (1995), 221–35.

(II) New Testament

M. Accad, 'Did the later Syriac Fathers take into consideration their Islamic context when reinterpreting the New Testament?', *Parole de l'Orient* 23 (1998), 13–32.

A. Baumstark, 'Die Evangelienexegese der syrischen Monophysiten', *Oriens Christianus* 2, 151–69, 358–89.

G. Beyer, 'Die evangelischen Fragen und Lösungen des Eusebius in jakobitischer Überlieferung und deren nestorianischen Parallelen', *Oriens Christianus* 20/22 (1925), 30–70; 23 (1927), 80–97, 284–92.

L. Brade, 'Die Herkunft von Prologen in den Paulusbriefexegesen des Theodoros bar Konai und Ishodad von Merv', *Oriens Christianus* 60 (1976), 162–71.

S. P. Brock, 'The Baptist's diet in Syriac sources', Oriens Christianus 54 (1970), 113–24; repr. in *From Ephrem to Romanos. Interactions between Syriac and Greek in Late Antiquity* (Variorum Reprints, Aldershot, 1999), Ch. X.

———, 'A neglected witness to the East Syrian New Testament commentary tradition: Sinai Ar. ms 151', in R. Ebied and H. Teule (eds.), *Studies on the Christian Arabic Heritage* (Eastern Christian Studies 5; Leuven, 2004), 205–15.

J. F. Coakley, 'The Old Man Simeon (Luke 2, 25) in Syriac tradition', *Orientalia Christiana Periodica* 47 (1981), 189–212.

R. Cowley, 'Scholia of Ahob of Qatar on St John's Gospel and the Pauline Epistles', *Le Muséon* 93 (1980), 329–43.

J. D. Hofstra, 'Isho' bar Nun's Questions and Answers on the Gospel of John and their relation to the Commentary of Isho'dad of Merv and Theodore bar Koni's Scholion', *VIIIth Symposium Syriacum = Journal of Eastern Christian Studies* 56 (2004), 69–94.

G. J. Reinink, *Studien zur Quellen- und Traditionsgeschichte des Evangelienkommentars der Gannat Bussame* (CSCO Subs. 57; 1979).

———, 'Die Exegese des Theodor von Mopsuestia in einem Anonymen nestorianischen Kommentar zum NT', *Studia Patristica* 19 (1989), 381–91.

VII. ASPECTS OF RECEPTION HISTORY (see Part I, Ch. 6–8)

(1) Narrative Poems

The Syriac text of most of these can be found in S. Brock (ed.), *Luqoto d-mimre d-'al ktobay qudsho/Eight Syriac Mimre on Biblical Themes* (Bar-Hebraeus Verlag, 1993).

Abraham and Sarah (Gen. 12): ed., with English tr., S. P. Brock and
S. Hopkins, *Le Muséon* 105 (1992), 87–146.
Abraham, Sarah and Isaac (two poems; Gen. 22): ed., with English tr.,
S. P. Brock, *Le Muséon* 99 (1986), 61–129; repr. in *From Ephrem to
Romanos* (Variorum Reprints, Aldershot, 1999), Ch. VI.
Joseph and his brothers (1) 12 poems attributed to Ephrem or Balai:
ed. P. Bedjan (1891).
Joseph and his brothers (2) 4 poems attributed to Narsai: ed. P. Bedjan
(1901); English tr. of two by A. S. Rodrigues Pereira, *Jaarbericht Ex
Oriente Lux* 31 (1989/90), 95–120.
Elijah and the Widow of Sarepta: ed., with English tr., S. P. Brock, *Le
Muséon* 102 (19890, 93–113; tr. also in *The Harp* 3:1/2 (1990), 75–
86.
Jonah (by Ephrem): ed. E. Beck, CSCO Scr. Syri 134–5; 1970 (*Sermones
II.1*); English tr. by H. Burgess, *The Repentance of Nineveh* (London,
1853).
Mary and Joseph: ed. in *Luqoto*; English tr. in S. Brock, *Bride of Light*
(Moran Etho 6; Kottayam, 1994).
The Sinful Woman (Luke 7; attributed to Ephrem): ed. E. Beck, *Sermones
II.4*; English tr. in Brock, *Bride of Light*.

(2) Verse Homilies

A large proportion of the verse homilies (memre) by Narsai , Jacob of
Serugh and (to a lesser extent) the various Isaacs are on biblical topics. The
list below is confined to those which have been translated:

(a) Narsai

Creation: ed., with French tr., Ph. Gignoux (Patrologia Orientalis 34;
1968).
Various: ed., with English tr., J. Frishman, *The Ways and Means of the
Divine Economy. Six Biblical Homilies by Narsai* (Diss. Leiden,
1992). [Enoch and Elijah, the Flood, Noah's Blessings, the
Tower of Babel, the Temporal Tabernacle, the Brazen Serpent].
Parables: ed., with French tr., E. P. Siman, *Narsai. Cinque homélies sur
les paraboles évangéliques* (Paris, 1984) [Ten Virgins, Prodigal Son,
Dives and Lazarus, the Workers in the Vineyard, the Good
Seed and the Tares]. Italian tr. of Wise and Foolish Virgins: M.
Nin (Monastero di Bose, 1997).

(b) Jacob of Serugh

Various indexes to Jacob's memre will be found in the additional vol. VI of the reprint (2006), by Gorgias Press, of P. Bedjan's edition of Jacob's verse homilies; the numbers in square brackets represent the homily number in Bedjan's edition; those with 'VI' are included in vol. VI.

Abbreviations: Kollamparampil = T. Kollamparampil, Jacob of Serugh. Select Festal Homilies (Rome/Bangalore, 1997); Landersdorfer = S. Landersdorfer, Ausgewählte Schriften der Syrischen Dichter (Kempten, 1912). Translations are in English unless otherwise stated.

Creation [71]: French tr. (excerpts) T. Jansma, *L'Orient Syrien* 4 (1959), 3–42, 129–62, 253–84.

First Day [71a]: tr. R. Darling, in J. W. Trigg, *Message of the Fathers* IX (1988), 184–202.

Creation (4 *memrè*): ed., with French tr., Kh. Alwan (CSCO Scr. Syri 214–5; 1989).

Melkizedeq [41]: tr. J. Thekeparampil, *The Harp* 6 (1993), 53–64.

Melkizedek [155]: tr. Anon., *The True Vine* 2 (1989), 30–55.

Abraham [109]: tr. R. E. McCarron, *Hugoye* 1:1 (1998).

Betrothal of Rebecca: French tr., F. Graffin, *L'Orient Syrien* 3 (1958), 324–36.

Jacob at Bethel [74]: French tr. F. Graffin, *L'Orient Syrien* 5 (1960), 227–46; German tr. in Landersdorfer, 332–43.

Rachel and Leah [75]: tr. Anon., *The True Vine* 4:4 (1993), 50–64.

Tamar (Gen. 38) [VI.12]: ed., with English tr., S. P. Brock, *Le Muséon* 115 (2002), 279–315.

Moses' Veil [79]: tr. S. P. Brock, *Sobornost/Eastern Churches Review* 3 (1981), 72–84; French tr. O. Rousseau, *La vie spirituelle* 91 (1954), 142–56; German tr. in Landersdorfer, 344–60; Dutch tr. A. Welkenhuysen, 1983, 1994).

The Two Sparrows [76]: French tr. F. Graffin, *L'Orient Syrien* 6 (1961), 54–66.

The Two Goats [78]: tr. D. Lane, *The Harp* 18 (2005), 365–91.

Red Heifer [77]: tr. D. Lane, *The Harp* 15 (2002), 35–42.

Bronze Serpent [4]: tr. Anon., *The True Vine* 6 (1990), 38–56.

Samson [160]: tr. Anon., *The True Vine* 11 (1992), 51–70.

Elijah [112–115]: French tr. in *Le saint prophète Élie* (Spiritualité Orientale 53; 1992), 484–604.

Elisha [116–121]: French tr. in *Le saint prophète Élisée* (Spiritualité Orientale 59; 1993), 249–363; English tr. of [117], Anon., *The True Vine* 1 (1989), 51–67.

Elisha's bones [35]: French tr. in *Le saint prophète Élisée*, 365–82.

Hosea: ed., with German tr., W. Strothmann (GOFS 5; 1973).

Nebuchadnezzar's madness [124]: tr. M. Henze, *The Madness of Nebuchadnezzar* (Leiden, 1999), 251–69.

Annunciation [VI.2]: tr. M. Hansbury, *Jacob of Serug. On the Mother of God* (Crestwood NY, 1998), 43–64.

Visitation [VI.3]: tr. Hansbury, *On the Mother of God*, 65–88.

Nativity of Christ [VI.6–8]: tr. in Kollamparampil, 41–127.

Baptism of Christ [8]: tr. in Kollamparampil, 159–86.

Entry to Temple [165]: tr. in Kollamparampil, 138–58.

Parables: Kingdom as Leaven [86]: tr. Anon., *The True Vine* 3 (1989), 44–57.

Parables: Prodigal Son [12]: tr. Anon., *The True Vine* 5:4 (1994), 11–37.

Parables: Pharisee and Publican 13]: tr. Anon., *The True Vine* 9 (1991), 19–34.

Parables: Ten Virgins [50]: tr. Anon., *The True Vine* 4:1 (1992), 39–62.

The Sinful Woman [51]: tr. S. F. Johnson, *Sobornost/Eastern Churches Review* 24 (2002), 56–88.

Transfiguration [49]: tr. in Kollamparampil, 201–30; French tr. E. Khoury, *Parole de l'Orient* 15 (1988/9), 65–90.

Entry to Jerusalem [18]: English tr. in Kollamparampil, 246–60.

Repentant thief [52]: German tr. in Landersdorfer, 360–74.

Resurrection [54–55]: tr. in Kollamparampil, 292–317.

Thomas [57]: tr. Anon., *The True Vine* 10 (1991), 57–73.

Ascension [VI.9]: tr. in Kollamparampil, 327–52.

Pentecost [58]: tr. in Kollamparampil, 353–69; German tr. in Landersdorfer, 271–85.

Stephen [98]: tr. Anon., *The True Vine* 7 (1990), 43–54.

(3) Dialogue Poems

The Syriac text of these can be found in S. Brock, *Sughyotho mgabyotho* (Monastery of St Ephrem, 1982).

Pishon and Jordan: ed., with English tr., S. P. Brock, *Parole de l'Orient* 23 (1998), 3–12.

Cain and Abel (2 poems): ed., with English tr., S. P. Brock, *Le Muséon* 113 (2000), 333–75.

Abraham and Isaac: English tr., S. P. Brock, *The Harp* 7 (1994), 55–72.

Joseph and Potiphar's wife: English tr. in S. P. Brock, *Treasurehouse of Mysteries* (forthcoming).

Joseph and his Brothers: ed., with English tr., S. P. Brock, in the Festschrift for R. Ebied (ed. P. Hill), forthcoming.

Zechariah and the Angel: English tr. in Brock, *Treasurehouse of Mysteries* (forthcoming).

Mary and the Angel: English tr. in Brock, *Bride of Light* (Moran Etho 6; Kottayam, 1994).

Mary and Joseph: English tr. in Brock, *Bride of Light*.

Mary and the Magi: English tr. in Brock, *Bride of Light*.

John the Baptist and Christ: English tr. in Brock, *Treasurehouse of Mysteries* (forthcoming).

The Sinful Woman (Luke 7) and Satan (2 poems): ed. with English tr., S. P. Brock, *Oriens Christianus* 72 (1988), 21–62; tr. of first also in *Sobornost/Eastern Churches Review* 13:2 (1992), 33–44.

The Two Thieves on the cross: English tr., S. P. Brock, in the Festschrift for J. Thekeparampil, (ed. B. Varghese and T. Koonammakkal), forthcoming.

The Cherub and the Thief (Luke 23:43): ed. with English tr., S. P. Brock in *Hugoye* 5:2 (2002), 169–93; ed. with Italian tr., F. A. Pennachietti, *Il Ladrone e il Cherubino. Dramma liturgico cristiano orientale in siriaco e neoramaico* (Torino, 1993).

Mary and the Gardener: ed., with English tr., S. P. Brock, *Parole de l'Orient* 11 (1983), 223–34; tr. also in *Bride of Light*.

(4) Studies

S. P. Brock, 'The Mysteries hidden in the side of Christ', *Sobornost* VII.6 (1978), 462–72.

———, 'Dramatic dialogue poems', *IV Symposium Syriacum* (Orientalia Christiana Analecta 229; 1987), 135–47.

———, 'Syriac Dispute Poems: the various types', in G. J. Reinink and H. L. J. Vanstiphout (eds.), *Dispute Poems and Dialogues in the Ancient and Medieval Mear East* (Orientalia Lovaniensia Analecta 42 (1991), 109–19; repr. in *From Ephrem to Romans* (Variorum Reprint, Aldershot, 1999), Ch. VII.

————, 'Fire from heaven: from Abel's sacrifice to the Eucharist', *Studia Patristica* 25 (1993), 229–43; repr. in *Fire from Heaven: Studies in Syriac Theology and Liturgy* (Variorum Reprints, Aldershot, 2006), Ch. V.

————, 'From Annunciation to Pentecost: the travels of a technical term [aggen]', in E. Carr and others (eds.), *Eulogema. Studies in Honor of Robert Taft S.J.* (Studia Anselmiana 110; Rome, 1993), 71–91; repr. in *Fire from Heaven*, Ch. XIII.

————, 'Ephrem's verse homily on Jonah and the Repentance of Nineveh', in A. Schoors and P. van Deun (eds.), *Polyhistor. Miscellanea in honorem Caroli Laga* (Orientalia Lovaniensia Analecta 60; 1994), 71–86; repr. in *From Ephrem to Romanos*, Ch. V.

————, 'The *ruah elohim* of Gen. 1,2 and its reception history in the Syriac tradition', in J-M. Auwers and A. Wénin (eds.), *Lectures et relectures de la Bible. Festschrift P.-M. Bogaert* (Leuven, 1999), 327–49; repr. in *Fire from Heaven*, Ch. XIV.

————, 'The Robe of Glory: a biblical image in the Syriac tradition', *Spirituality and Clothing = The Way* 39 (1999), 247–59.

————, 'The background to some terms in the Syriac Eucharistic epicleses', *The Harp* 13 (2000), 1–12.

————, ' The Dispute poem: from Sumer to Syriac', *Journal of the Canadian Society for Syriac Studies* 1 (2001), 3–20.

————, 'Dinah in a Syriac poem on Joseph', in G. Khan (ed.), *Semitic Studies in Honour of Edward Ullendorff* (Leiden, 2005), 222–35.

————, 'The Bridal Chamber of Light: a distinctive feature of the Syriac liturgical tradition', *The Harp* 18 (2005), 179–91.

————, 'The use of the Syriac versions in the liturgy', forthcoming in MPIL.

————, 'Radical renunciation: the ideal of *msarrquta*', forthcoming in R. Darling Young (ed.), Festschrift for S. H. Griffith.

A. Golitzin, 'The image and glory of God in Jacob of Serugh's Homily 'On that Chariot that Ezekiel the Prophet saw', *St Vladimir's Seminary Theological Review* 47:3/4 (2003), 323–64.

S. A. Harvey, 'Why the perfume mattered: the Sinful Woman in Syriac exegetical tradition', in P. M. Blowers and others (eds.), *In Dominico Eloquio. In Lordly Eloquence: Essays in Patristic Exegesis in Honor of R. L. Wilken* (Grand Rapids, 2002), 69–89.

————, 'On Mary's voice: gendered words in Syriac Marian tradition', in D. B. Martin and P. Cox Miller (eds.), *The Cultural Turn in Late Ancient Studies* (Durham NC, 2005), 63–86.

K. S. Heal, 'Joseph as a type of Christ in Syriac literature', *Brigham Young University Studies* 42:1 (2002), 29–49.

D. Lane, 'The use of Psalms in five Syriac authors', in A. Rapoport-Albert and G. Greenberg (eds.), *Biblical Hebrew/Biblical Texts* (Sheffield, 2001), 412–30.

R. Murray, 'Aramaic and Syriac dispute poems and their connections', in M. J. Geller, J. C. Greenfield, and M. Weitzman (eds.), *Studia Aramaica* (Journal of Semitic Studies, Supplement 4; 1995), 157–87.

L. Wehbé, 'Textes bibliques dans les écrits de Martyrius-Sahdona', *Melto* 5 (1969), 61–112.